# WRITE
# FICTION
# WITHOUT
# THE FUSS

# HOW TO WRITE FICTION WITHOUT THE FUSS

## LUCY McCARRAHER

# R3THINK PRESS

First published in 2013 by Rethink Press
(www.rethinkpress.com)

*To all fiction writers past, present and especially future – whose dedication to their craft has and will bring their unique stories to readers everywhere.*

# THANKS TO...

Anthony Wagner, my late father, who read me a wide variety of fiction, including *Pride and Prejudice* when I was eight, the ghost stories of M. R. James (notably the nightmare-inducing 'The Tractate Middoth'), the Victorian epic *Adventures of Tim Pippin,* and classical myths from *The Golden Bough.* An avid reader of fiction and lucid writer himself, he taught me that taking the easy route in reading or writing is not always the best way.

Suzan St Maur, who asked me to write a series on Fiction Writing for her amazing writers' website, *www.howtowritebetter.net*, and thus forced me to write the basis of this book. She also chose the title.

Barbara Levy, literary agent, to whom I refer to in the Introduction, who gave me an invaluable, if unwelcome at the time, lesson in fiction writing.

Ellen Graham, Robert Warren Bell, Keble Howard and Betty Askwith, novelists and my great grandmother, great uncles and great aunt respectively, whose story-telling genes may have been passed on to me.

My Creative Writing and Adult Literacy tutors and students at City College Norwich, where I took my

Diploma in Teaching in the Lifelong Learning Sector, who all taught me how to elucidate aspects of writing, editing, grammar and punctuation.

All the fiction writers I have worked with, and whose books I have worked on, as an editor, coach and publisher.

# PRAISE

'As the perpetrator here, I cheerfully plead *mea culpa* to having shoved Lucy's arm up her back and made her write the amazing series on which this book is based... and I think both she and I are glad I did! Her series was easily the most popular on *HowToWriteBetter.net* and still has thousands of "reads" every week. When you consider how much complex and stuffy information is dribbling around the internet (and in bookshops) on how to write fiction, Lucy's clear, concise and unfussy advice is a Godsend. Read it, read it again, follow it to the letter and your fiction is bound to flower and bear fruit.'

Suzan St Maur, author of 'How To Write Winning Non-fiction' and 31 other published books

'This book does exactly what it says in the title: it gives you the tools to write fiction, from the first word to sending out your manuscript. This book is just what I've been looking for when teaching Creative Writing. Its clear, no-nonsense approach urges the reader to get writing, as it is coupled with very practical exercises, has inspirational quotes to keep you going, and is sufficiently comprehensive to get you to the end of your novel. The book is useful for those starting out on their novel-writing journey and the checklists are a suitable *aide memoire* for more experienced writers. One of the best 'How to' books on writing I've come across.'

Amanda Addison, author of 'Laura's Handmade Life'; co-author of the UK's first Access to HE in Creative Writing course; Creative Writing tutor at City College Norwich

'In *How To Write Fiction*, Lucy McCarraher has distilled all her common sense, wisdom and experience into a concise, readable and practical guide to anyone embarking on the daunting and terrifying task of writing a novel. Not only do I appreciate the book as a novelist, but am also inclined to steal her ideas wholesale as a Creative Writing teacher!'

Sarah Bower, author of 'The Needle In The Blood' and the international bestseller, 'Sins of the House of Borgia'

'A book of great wisdom and great practicality. Here are the things we need to know, possibly think we know and, when we need them most, realise we don't. Lucy points out that, of course, in writing fiction inspiration and creativity are vital, but necessarily in tandem with a thorough understanding of structure, storyline, grammar and punctuation. This she provides in an easily accessible and enjoyable text. She takes her own advice, for example, in showing more than telling: each point is aptly illustrated from a wide range of novels.

'We all need reminders of the way to go, and here are the essential indicators. I found one good and true thing after another. A book to go back to over and over, and gain from each time.'

James Ferron Anderson, award-winning author of 'The River And The Sea'

'As a published non-fiction author with an ambition to write good fiction, I am an instant fan of this book. It makes it clear that to work, fiction needs to be planned, crafted and polished until it is perfect.

'There are lots of invaluable tips on grammar and punctuation which would benefit most of us. What particularly stood out for me was the advice on grabbing the readers' attention, developing the plot and "showing" rather than "telling". I will add this to my dictionary and thesaurus as an indispensable writing aid.'

Geoffrey Salmon, author of 'Kendo: A Comprehensive Guide to Japanese Swordsmanship' and 'Kendo – Inherited Wisdom'

'I am a writer who constantly strives to hone my craft and *How to Write Fiction* by Lucy McCarraher has become one of my most useful tools. With only the bare bones of a plot, the sketch of a character to work with, Lucy takes you through the development of outlining plots and developing characters. She takes the novelist right though to final edits and submitting your work. I feel comfortable with Lucy's methods, the book is easy to read, great to dip in an out of and I have found that not only my writing, but my thought processes have improved. All writers need a mentor and having this book on my e-reader I really feel that I have my own personal writing coach with me.'

Michelle Heatley is a published short story writer and her debut novel 'Fish Soup' is soon to be published. She has a Diploma in Literature and Creative Writing from the Open University.

'A must read for anyone contemplating writing a novel. *How To Write Fiction* guides you through all of the stages involved in becoming an author, helping with plot, structure and grammar through to approaching agents and publishers, and all written in an easy to read, yet informative style. With so many handy tips on offer, I defy even the most seasoned of author not to find something of use within this book's pages.'

**Keri Beevis, award winning author of 'Dead Letter Day'**

# CONTENTS

## INTRODUCTION

## PART ONE: PREPARATION

## PART TWO: WRITING

## PART THREE: REVIEWING & EDITING

## PART FOUR: GETTING PUBLISHED

## ABOUT THE AUTHOR

# INTRODUCTION

As a writer and author I have worked in many genres and formats over the years. I've been a journalist and reviewer; I've written TV scripts and outlines; business and research reports and manuals; self-development books and novels.

I'm also an editor and publisher who has worked on manuscripts, and with authors, of all kinds. There's no genre of writing I don't enjoy, but for me fiction, and the novel especially – to both read and write – is the ultimate art form, educational tool, emotional resource, entertainment medium and guilty pleasure.

If you've ever wanted to try your hand at fiction, started a novel or short story, or completed a manuscript but think it lacks a certain something, then stick with me. This book looks at all aspects of the craft of fiction writing, and aims to give you a clear understanding of the fundamentals along with tools and tips to enhance your writing proficiency.

My first attempt at a novel was a thinly disguised tale of part of my own life. I sent it to an agent who told me it was (a) boring and (b) unbelievable. It was too contrived, she said, to have a novel about families with a central character who was a family researcher, whose mother was the director of a children's charity and whose father was a genealogist. 'But it can't be unbelievable,' I whined. 'It's true!'

'Truth and fiction are not the same thing,' she snapped.

I'd like to help you not make the same mistake I did in assuming that life provides stories ready made for fiction. It doesn't. I learned my lesson and my next attempt at fiction was put together around the information I have collated for you in this book. *Blood and Water* was short-listed from 47,000 entries to the Richard and Judy How To Be Published competition and published by Macmillan New Writing.

You don't have to commit to writing a novel to be a fiction writer: you can tell a micro-story in a few hundred words; a short story in a few thousand; a novelette would take you up to 20,000 words, while a novella would be a little longer, but shorter than a full length novel. Once you get beyond 200,000 words, you've written an epic!

All types of fiction, though, require their writers to address the key elements: story and theme; plot and exposition; character delineation and development;

setting and season; climax and anti-climax; action and resolution; not to mention genre, niche and writing style. We will look at all these in more detail and why you need to be aware of them in order to position your work, and present it professionally for publication and the right readership.

Although inspiration and creativity are vital factors in the art of writing fiction, they are for you to develop in your own way. The only advice I would give you on this is to read: read mostly good, but also bad fiction, and note how it is done well. Read the genre and format you want to write in, and find their limits by reading other work outside them. Read, mark, learn and inwardly digest.

## 'Writing comes from reading, and reading is the finest teacher of how to write.'
### E. ANNIE PROULX

It is just as important, though, to understand the craft – even science – of story-writing, from structure and storyline through to grammar and punctuation, in spinning the threads of your imagined world. That is where this book can help you.

Before, though, you even set pen to paper (or finger to key, more likely), you must take the time to think, to dream, to imagine... Some writers take a year or more to allow their creative juices to bubble around their central story, the lives of their characters and the world they inhabit. This internal development is the first step to creating a strong work of fiction and is not one that can be skipped.

If you are setting out on your novel or short story, start to form in your mind the parallel universe that will become your creative writing. Get into the habit of living in that place, time and environment whenever you're alone, doing a mundane task, walking or travelling (warning: be careful when driving or operating machinery). Remember that your subconscious has access to a mass of information your conscious mind does not, so set it on autopilot. When it needs supplementing, your library and the internet contain the rest – and we will be looking at the topic of research in fiction.

'Tell the story that's been growing in your heart, the characters you can't keep out of your head, the tale story that speaks to you, that pops into your head on your daily commute, that wakes you up in the morning.'

JENNIFER WEINER

From now until you know the time is right, don't write a thing. Just use that very powerful mechanism, your brain, to start the creative process that will become your work of fiction.

While this is happening, or if you are already mid-manuscript or polishing a final draft, now is the time to ensure you have all the tools of the trade at your disposal to produce the most professional work you can.

# PART ONE

# PREPARATION

**1**

# OUTLINING YOUR PLOT AND STRUCTURE

After the process of immersing yourself internally in your characters, setting and story – sometimes evocatively referred to as 'composting', and only you can know when you've done enough composting – it's time to take the first step in externalising your work.

One barrier to getting started on a novel is fear of the blank page, the empty book stretching ahead… Another is the mistaken belief that creative writing should only be inspired and free-flowing. On the contrary, most successful writers plan, plot and structure first to create a flexible frame and gripping narrative for their characters and setting, and this first exercise helps overcome both these barriers.

> 'When the writer… says he has worked without giving any thought to the process, he simply means he was working without realizing he knew the rules.'
>
> UMBERTO ECO

Each writer develops their own preferred method and order of planning. Some of you may prefer to start with Characters or Setting – which will be coming up shortly – but we're going jump in with the Plot. Some people differentiate story and plot on the basis that **The Story** is the events and actions in your novel – 'and then… and then…' – while **The Plot** is about cause and effect, why things happen and characters act as they do – 'because… because…'. I'm going to combine both, in this first exercise, under the term **Plot**.

Underlying most good fiction are two structural principles:

- the **Three Act** form, which breaks down the narrative into Beginning, Middle and End; and

- the **Story Arc**, a framework that can be simple or complex, but should successfully draw the reader through almost any kind of plot or genre.

The Story Arc can be summarised as:

- **The Trigger**, the inciting action or event which sets off

- **The Quest** (anything, from finding love, crossing a continent, to unmasking a murderer); The Quest involves one to three

- **Reversals**, each progressively more detrimental to achieving the goal of The Quest; but lead (often surprisingly) to

- **The Climax** – when understanding is achieved; and finally

- **Resolution**, where the last threads are untangled and loose ends tied up.

With these in mind, we will use a simple tool to create the outline structure of your work of fiction – a **One-page Overview**. Whether you're a list-maker, a mind-mapper or box-filler, design on a single page a numbered, eight-chapter structure. (You can later divide these into 12, 24 or any other number of chapters – or none at all.)

Group Chapters 1 and 2 under the heading **Beginning**, Chapters 3 to 6 under **Middle,** and 7 and 8 as **End**.

Head the chapters:

1. **Trigger**

2. **Quest Begins**

3. **Quest Continues**

4. **Reversal 1**

5. **Reversal 2**

6. **Reversal 3**

7. **Climax**

8. **Resolution**

Summarise under each chapter, in a few sentences, the elements of your plot that fit the headings. Try and ensure that events in the Beginning two chapters are setting up the main action; that the Middle four chapters contain a rise and fall of events that become increasingly tense; and that the two End chapters bring clarity and resolve (if not a happy ending).

How long each element takes to unfold will depend on how you write it at a later date, but this overview will provide you with an initial view of your novel structure and offer the chance to check whether the flow of events fits with a classic, tried and tested fiction format.

This exercise may sound simple, but to get the balance of your plot right may take a little more work that you expected.

**2**

# DEVELOPING YOUR CHARACTERS

With an overview of your plot in place, let's work on the most important element of any piece of fiction: the characters. Every other aspect of your story – plot, theme, genre, exposition, engagement – depends on the characters you create to wrap them around. They are the single element that will keep your readers absorbed; even one believable, fascinating character that inhabits their imagination can make up for less than perfect plotting or writing style.

Think back to any memorable novel, story, film or TV series and see if it wasn't one or two of the main characters who kept you reading or viewing, stayed with you long after the end, and who you still see, hear, love or hate in your head, even if you've forgotten the details of the plot.

A key step to creating such characters is the 'composting' process I talked about earlier. It is vital to spend time living imaginatively with your cast before committing them to paper, letting each one take shape over time, growing from a look or single trait into a rounded personality with a life of their own. Often, your main protagonists will have introduced themselves as the starting point of your novel or short story; surrounding or lesser characters may take longer to materialise.

To build a credible character, you could start from someone you know, from life, the media or other fiction, making sure they grow into an original creation as you envisage them in your own settings. Never leave a character recognisable as a real person – for legal as well as creative reasons! Alternatively, start from an archetype – heroine, villain, confidante, trickster – or a plot requirement – jealous ex, interfering parent – and gather physical and emotional traits around this.

**"Every human being has hundreds of separate people living under his skin. The talent of a writer is his ability to give them their separate names, identities, personalities and have them relate to other characters living with him.'**

MEL BROOKS

Although the details may not play a part in your story, you, the writer, must know all your main characters' 'back stories': where they were born, grew up and were educated; how they were raised in what kind of family; the key emotional events in their lives before they arrived at your starting point. All these will have produced the attitude, motivation, purpose and detail which are essential to writing a convincing character.

Whether you have all this material at your fingertips, or feel stuck on some areas, the next section of your story's 'bible' is getting your characters into written form. Characters aren't robots: you don't design and build them then expect them to perform a function; they must be people who develop organically through their own actions, reactions and interactions. This exercise, though, will give you a solid grounding from which to further build your plot and storyline.

Whether you are writing your fiction 'bible' on paper or electronically, start a new section headed **Characters**. Assign a page to each main character, headed by their name, and perhaps half a page to each lesser character (don't get carried away by detail at this point). Depending on the structure of your work, you might want to group them in subsections such as Main Plot, Sub-plot 1, Sub-plot 2; or in different families or settings. The more order you bring to your 'bible' now, the more clarity it will offer when you start writing.

Give each character a factual background: date of birth, place of upbringing, family of origin, education, dates of key life events (marriage, trauma, career achievements...) their current home and environment; and brief physical description, although this is less important to readers than you may imagine, they will always create their own picture. If possible, assign them an archetype (see above). Follow this information with a one-line description of their role in your story, such as 'Main protagonist, unwilling seeker of truth about his mother's murder, falls in love with X after initial dislike'. You can return to this succinct summary to keep your character and plot on track while writing.

After the facts, allow your imagination freedom to describe your character's emotional base – especially the motivation for their action and purpose in the story. You might want to note down a typical snatch of dialogue or scenario. Quirks are a great way of signposting them to the reader, such as turns of phrase, beliefs, habits or tics – although don't let these become clichés or excuses for real characterisation later.

Keep these descriptions to the suggested length to clarify and focus your thoughts and keep your full creative powers for the story itself. The activity of writing these descriptions will clarify not just your individual cast members, but their role and function in the plot and in relation to other characters.

'The only thing worth writing about is people. People. Human beings. Men and women whose individuality must be created line by line, insight by insight. If you do not do it, the story is a failure.'

HARLAN ELLISON

**3**

# CREATING THE SETTING

Along with plot, character, style and theme, the **setting** is a key element in a piece of fiction. Authors and critics have called a novel's setting a 'character in its own right' and, while it doesn't have to play a dynamic role in every story, without a realistic and specific backdrop your characters will seem pallid and amorphous and your plot will lack credibility.

Consider just three classic writers and what their novels would be like without their settings: Charles Dickens, Armistead Maupin and JK Rowling. The stories of *David Copperfield* or *Oliver Twist* would be hollow without the backdrop and context of 19th century London; San Francisco rightly takes top billing in the title of *Tales of the City*; and the imaginary world of Hogwarts School creates magic for the reader in more than the obvious sense.

So what do these three – and all other successful – authors include in their settings to make them so involving?

Firstly, whether they are 'real' or fantastical, each of their fictional worlds are highly *specific*. Just as they know their characters inside out, the authors bring detailed knowledge and description of the *places* their characters move through.

Setting is not, though, just about location. It is also about historical *period* and the society, ethos and culture that pertain to that time. They are how we understand the way characters think and behave, and the factors that drive them. Dickens' period characters do not share the moral outlook – or indeed dialogue style – of Maupin's '70s hippies.

Other aspects of your setting that influence plot and characters are its geography and/or architecture and decor, social class, weather, season and time of day. These can be used to underline, or counterpoint, narrative moods and can provide metaphorical resonance for your theme.

If your entire novel or short story is set in one location, your job may be simpler than if you choose multiple locations for different plot elements. Your work will be different, too, if your setting is contemporary rather than historical: in either case you may already know or be able to visit the district, or you will need to do the appropriate research to bring it to life for readers (who may know the place or time themselves and won't appreciate errors).

A totally invented world will need all the elements mentioned above – though it might, like *Harry Potter,* overlap with and provide a commentary on the world we know. If you are creating an imagined setting, the most important thing to remember is *consistency.* The environment needs to be meticulously thought through in every detail, even if they don't all appear in the story, and to remain coherent from start to finish.

To help you do this, open a new section in your fiction 'bible' called **Settings** and head a page for each location. Make sub-headings for:

**Environment** – make notes on the landscape or cityscape: the natural geography, buildings – exterior and interior, layout of streets or countryside, wildlife, human inhabitants, social class… You might want to consider how these settings affect your characters – do they brutalise or sensitise; do they love or hate their environments? Use all four senses to fully imagine and describe your environment.

**Period and Context** – even if your setting is contemporary or imagined, take the time to identify the current social and political attitudes. Think about gender positions, outlook on the issues of your story, real life events, methods of transport and communication. If you are writing in multiple time schemes, you will need a heading for each, comparing and contrasting important aspects.

**Season** – clarify the time(s) of year in which your story takes place, how this impacts on the landscape and the action, reflects or adds irony to your characters' feelings. Make notes on specific weather conditions you could use; months, days of the week, times of day that your plot draws on and the effect they might have.

**Research** – what is missing from the above that you need to know, and where will you find it? It might be tiny details or a major exploration that needs to be undertaken to fill the gaps. We will look at this activity in more detail shortly.

If there are aspects specific to the settings in your story that require more examination – particularly if you are inventing a new world – add other headings.

**4**

# DEFINING YOUR THEME

Now you have the outlines of your plot, characters and setting in place, it's time to explore the theme – or themes – of your novel or short story.

**The theme** is the central idea(s) which underlies a work of fiction. It is nothing so crude as a 'message' (which, if too obvious, will detract from good creative writing), but combines the wisdom, the moral, the paradigm or thesis you explore within your story.

The greatest novels include a number of inter-related themes: Jane Austen's *Pride and Prejudice*, for instance, manages to look at marriage, gender politics, property, class and social hypocrisy within an apparently light-hearted comedy of manners. But an over-arching theme linking all the others is that love overcomes pride (and prejudice).

In *To Kill A Mockingbird*, Harper Lee examines love for people, the importance of living things and tolerance of others' beliefs – but the key theme is southerners' lack of acceptance of black emancipation.

You may start your story with one theme in mind and find that others emerge as you progress. You might not even recognise an issue you have addressed until you come to revise and edit your work. The value of distinguishing themes at this stage is that they provide you with a structure for sharpening the relevant and cutting the unnecessary elements of your story.

Some novelists claim not to think about theme before writing; they prefer to concentrate on telling a good story and see what emerges. However, every writer has interests, opinions, biases and attitudes, whether conscious or unconscious, which influence what they write; whether you are aware of them or not, your own experience and knowledge create themes in your work.

It makes sense, then, to focus on this aspect of your story at the outset and actively to make use of it. Not to do so can produce some unintended and unwanted consequences: if you are a less experienced writer and pursue your plot without keeping an eye on your underlying theme, it could materialise as trite, passé or overly 'messagey'; equally, without holding a theme in mind, you might leave your readers confused by characters and events that lack a coherent authorial perspective.

If you have come to this project with an issue you want to explore, you need to make sure your novel expresses what you want it to. Most importantly, though, a solid thematic structure is a major organising force in fiction, giving it depth, resonance and emotional impact. A well-developed theme is as valuable to your novel as character and plot.

Start a new page in your project 'bible' and head it **Theme**. If you already know your main theme, summarise it in a single sentence. If you are also able, add sentence-long summaries for your sub-themes – which should all have some link to the main theme.

If you are not yet clear about the theme(s) of your story, go back over your one-page plot outline and ask yourself:

- 'What does the reader know at the end of this story that they didn't know at the beginning?'

- 'What lessons emerge from the key incidents in this plot?'

- 'Where does the story highlight different sides of a single position?'

Read back over your character descriptions and enquire of each person:

- 'What do you learn as a result of your journey in this story?'

- 'What viewpoints do you represent – and does it change by the end?'

- 'Which other character(s) do you agree and disagree with, and what will the tension between you reveal to the reader?'

The answers to these questions may take some time to emerge but, as they do, make notes about them on your **Theme** page. Highlight key actions, interactions and events in the plot line. Makes notes of where the attitudes of different characters originate. Refer back to your notes on **Setting** and consider historical period and culture.

This is a good time, before you start writing, to clarify your themes and perhaps to tweak your plot outline and characters in response.

**5**

# RESEARCH

If fiction is a work of the imagination, why would you need research to write your story?

Because you want the reader to believe absolutely in your imaginative world and most fictional worlds have some relationship to the real world, as it was, is, or might be. Whatever your subject matter or setting, some of your readers will know or be well informed about it. Factual errors will spoil their reading experience and invite negative reviews.

So what are the key areas of research for fiction writers?

## Names

Remember to make sure something as basic as your characters' names fit with the period, setting and tenor of your story. Thinking about their names forces you to clarify the characters' backgrounds: what age, class and type of people were the parents who gave their child that name? The internet is an ideal place to find the origins, popularity, nationality and meanings of names.

## Location

The setting of your story is crucial to the feel, and possibly plotline, of your story. If you don't want to be tied to the specifics of a real place, you could consider inventing a fictional town, country or village (as I did in *Kindred Spirits*) based on some reality. But if you are going to set it in an existing location, make sure that all the details are accurate. I recently edited a new novel set in late 80s Chelsea, a time and place I knew well. The author and I worked on getting every tube journey, bus route, walk that the characters took, and descriptions of cafés, shops and buildings entirely accurate. To someone like me, who lived in London at that time, mistakes took me out of the story and diminished the reality.

Make sure you have the correct geography, seasons and weather of a setting you don't know well from personal experience. If you can't travel to see a place, the internet can give you maps, photos and sometimes videos of locations, in the past and present. You can also visit online, or talk to, tourism departments; safest, though, is to check with someone who has firsthand knowledge of the place.

## Careers

How does a small town cop relate to an FBI agent? Keri Beevis doesn't live in America, but had to research that relationship for her novel, *Dead Letter Day*. Her style and plot don't require procedural details of how US cops and Feds interact on a murder enquiry, so Keri gives an accurate minimum of technical information based on reading and online research, and concentrates on the central emotional relationship, leaving the reader enough space to imagine the rest.

There is information on the web, in the library, from businesses and organisations on almost any career or job one of your characters might have, but tracking down a real life member of the profession you are writing about can give unexpected and intriguing details that add interest and realism to your characters and plot.

## Historical period

This kind of research can be the most time-consuming – and many historical novelists have described the length and intensity of their work in this area. Immerse yourself in the period before you start writing: read research papers, history books, contemporary literature and diaries. For atmosphere, watch television dramas and documentaries as well as films – though check their accuracy against the facts. Listen to music and examine details of costume and decor in works of art and photographs (if you are working on more recent history) of the time. Newspapers and journals are an invaluable resource, not just for records and fact-finding, but also to enable you to get a feel for the language and attitudes of day.

In her World War One novel, *Rumour*, Angela Lawrence brings research further into her story than most fiction writers by including complete newspaper articles (one of her characters is a reporter) and basing courtroom scenes on transcripts. In the editing process, though, sections were pruned where too many facts slowed down the story.

## Language

If your story contains characters who come from a country, county, city or area you don't know well, you will need to research the way they talk. Not only must you have the appropriate words, terms and turns of phrase to make them sound credible, you will need a feel for the flow and rhythm of their speech. If possible, spend time with someone who comes from your character's location or background; if not, listen to dialogue in appropriate films or tv dramas (hoping the actors got it right –

don't take a lesson in Cockney English from Dick Van Dyke), or the speech of someone in the media who sounds like your character.

Creating dialogue for historical characters may have to be a mixture of research and imagination, with imagination taking precedence the further back in time you go. Received English in, for example, Tudor times, sounded like a regional accent of today, and used words and phrases unknown to us. Read literature of your chosen period to get a flavour, pick some contemporary vocabulary, then develop your own, consistent style of dialogue. Make sure it is not so arcane as to distract readers from  following the sense, and look out for obvious anachronisms. Differentiate each character's speech and (see the section on **Writing Dialogue**) don't start writing until you can clearly hear each voice in your head.

## Primary research

Some genres of fiction are heavily reliant on research. Crime fiction requires knowledge of criminal psychology, execution of the crime and investigative procedures. What makes any story succeed, though, is the emotional experience of the characters, so although you may need to read up on serial killers' modus operandi and forensic science, a day spent in a court gallery to watch real judges, lawyers, criminals and witnesses interacting will be invaluable. Makes notes of the sensations, sounds, smells, textures and emotional flavour of the day; see how the press, public and court staff behave. No amount of scientific information will keep a reader involved like being drawn into a fully-drawn, believable episode.

## Putting research into writing

Take notes while you are researching, to help you embed interesting, unusual and key facts, but put all your books, pamphlets and notebooks to one side when you start your first draft and let your imagination go to work on all the material you have absorbed. Check individual details you need to know for your plot, but wait until your second draft to adjust for complete accuracy. In your first draft give fiction free reign and concentrate on the emotions and experience of your characters.

Your plot and characters should always take precedence over your research; don't change your plot to include an amazing fact you discovered, and don't use your characters to give the reader (rather than each other) information so their dialogue sounds unnatural and stilted.

Use second and third drafts, and an editor's eye, to keep the balance right and prioritise fiction over fact – even if it sometimes means bending the truth a little. You can even have fun by using your research to add value for a minority of readers who will understand certain references, without compromising the story for the majority who will not.

# 6

# CLASSIFYING YOUR FORM

Whether you have started writing, or are still in the planning stages, it's important to be clear on what form of fiction you have been, or are considering, writing.

Prose fiction is usually divided into six categories, based on length. Why, you might ask, is there any need to classify your story according to its wordage; it's the creative process that matters first, followed by the enjoyment readers get from it, neither of which is dependent on the number of pages that have been filled or turned.

The answer is that even if you are writing purely for your own pleasure, inspiration is best channelled through the perspiration of form and structure. And if you are hoping for an audience, let alone representation and/or publication, you are more likely to find them by writing within the familiar forms that readers seek and publishers provide.

## Fiction formats

**Flash Fiction,** as its name suggests, is very short fiction. There is no widely accepted definition of the length, but some markets make 300 words the maximum while others go up to 2,000 words.

Paper publication of flash fiction stories is rare, but there are growing numbers of dedicated internet sites and zines, such as *www.flashfictiononline.com*, which run frequent competitions and publish winners.

**The Short Story** may be the most ancient form of fiction, originating in the oral tradition. Short stories are the most popular form of fiction competitions, and literary organisations and publishers request maximum lengths that can vary between 500 and 7,500 words. More generally, a short story is defined as between 2,000 words and 7,500 words. Short stories follow the same overall structure as longer fiction forms, but will probably minimise the central second act to a single, or two at most, reversals.

Short story anthologies by well-known writers are occasionally published, but rarely succeed commercially. Self-publishing and e-book publication, though, are generating a new market for short story writers, either in anthologies or even single stories.

> '*A short story is a love affair, a novel is a marriage. A short story is a photograph; a novel is a film.*'
>
> **LORRIE MOORE**

The term **Novelette** applies to a narrative work of prose fiction that is longer than a short story and shorter than a novella. That description makes it a story of at least 7,500 words but under 17,500 words. It can also, though, be used to refer to a short novella, especially one with a trivial or sentimental theme.

Novelettes are rarely traditionally published these days, but two long-standing awards for science fiction novelettes are the Hugo Awards and the Nebula Awards.

**A Novella**, then, is a work of at least 17,500 words but under 50,000 words. It too will generally feature fewer conflict points (or reversals) than a novel, but have a more complex plot than a short story. Unlike novels, novellas are not usually divided into chapters, and were once intended for reading at a single sitting. The shorter novella sticks with a main plot and a single point of view, but often has well developed characters and rich description.

You might be surprised to realise how many classic and famous works are novellas rather novels.

A handful are: John Steinbeck's *Of Mice and Men*, George Orwell's *Animal Farm*, Anthony Burgess' *A Clockwork Orange*, Isaac Asimov's *Nightfall*, Robert Louis Stevenson's *The Strange Case of Dr Jekyll and Mr Hyde*, Charles Dickens' *A Christmas Carol*, H. G. Wells' *The Time Machine*, Joseph Conrad's *Heart of Darkness* and Stephen King's *Rita Hayworth and Shawshank Redemption*.

As you can see from even this small selection, the novella form has long been favoured by writers of science fiction, futuristic and fantasy fiction. Novellas in these genres, and the sub-genre of steampunk, are currently thriving, especially in e-book form. There are Hugo and Nebula awards for novellas, along with others for fantasy, mystery, romance and literary fiction.

Robert Silverberg, in the introduction to the novella anthology, *Sailing to Byzantium*, said:

> (The novella) is one of the richest and most rewarding of literary forms... it allows for more extended development of theme and character than does the short story, without making the elaborate structural demands of the full-length book. Thus it provides an intense, detailed exploration of its subject, providing to some degree both the concentrated focus of the short story and the broad scope of the novel.

**The Novel** is, of course, the longest and most complex and perennially popular form of prose fiction, of 50,000 words or more. If you are trying to sell a first novel to an agent or publisher, 80,000 words is a good length to aim for, unless you are writing an Epic, in which case you will have to hit or pass the 200,000 word mark.

**Epics** are most often historical novels, like Margaret Mitchell's *Gone With The Wind* and Boris Pasternak's *Dr Zhivago*; generational family stories (John Galsworthy's *The Forsyte Saga*, Colleen McCullough's *The Thorn Birds*); or epic fantasies, such as J.R.R. Tolkein's *Lord of the Rings* and George R.R. Martin's *A Game of Thrones*.

Whatever length you plan your story, or the word count you reach by the end of it, try to ensure it fits the criteria and structure of the appropriate form, and seek the readership and means of publication most suited to it.

7

# IDENTIFYING YOUR GENRE

If format is one axis of the fiction matrix, genre is the other. Although, confusingly, 'genre fiction' is often used to describe popular, plot-driven, niche fiction (such as Romance or Mystery), I am talking about genre in its broader sense, as used by publishers and booksellers to classify all types of fiction.

If you want to sell your book into an agent or traditional publisher, you should know your fiction genre, the idioms of that genre, best-selling books and writers within it, and where your story fits in relation to these. Like it or not, purveyors of books like to market their wares under clear categories and if yours doesn't fit one, it's an easy reason for them to turn it down. Even self-publishers will need to specify the appropriate genre(s) for their books on Amazon.

Screenwriting guru, Robert McKee, usefully defines genre conventions as the 'specific settings, roles, events, and values that define individual genres and their subgenres.'

The two uber-genres of fiction, within one of which your writing should clearly sit, are *literary* and *commercial*.

**Literary fiction** tends to appeal to an educated and intellectually adventurous readership, owing to its high quality of writing, original content and developed style. Any of the subgenres below can be written in literary style, but they will have a different tone to the more popular versions. Literary fiction is what wins awards like the Booker and Orange prizes.

**Commercial fiction** attracts a broad audience and may also fall into any subject genre or sub-genre. 'Blockbuster' authors usually write commercial rather than literary fiction; typical commercial fiction authors are John Grisham, Jilly Cooper, Danielle Steele, E L James and Jackie Collins.

**Mainstream fiction** is a general term used by publishers and booksellers about both commercial and literary works that don't fit another genre and are usually set in the present, tell the stories of recognisable characters and have themes relevant to most people's lives. 'Contemporary realism' might be another description of mainstream fiction. Most bestseller novels are considered mainstream, although they include a wide range of authors.

The main fiction sub-genres are:

**Mystery** fiction generally focuses on a crime, often murder, or if not a crime, a secret that needs exposing. The action centres on the attempts of an actual detective, or character in that role for the purposes of the story, to solve the crime/mystery. The climax happens at the point of unraveling, where all the elements of the detective work neatly come together. The solution, complete with reversals and surprises, is finally delivered to the characters and the reader alike.

Sub-genres of mystery include spy, police, and family stories. Authors in this genre are as diverse as Arthur Conan Doyle, Raymond Chandler, Nicci French, Carl Hiaason and Sophie Hannah.

**Romance** is a massive genre, with women its main audience. Romance novels include varying elements of fantasy, love, sex and adventure, and always the heroic lover (male or female) overcoming the odds to be with their true love. Sub-genres can be formulaic: gothic romances, for example, follow the formula of a young, inexperienced girl living somewhere remote, being courted or threatened by an evil man and then rescued by a valiant one.

Other sub-genres include historical, holiday, contemporary, erotic, comedy (rom com) and fantasy romance. If historical detail and settings interest you, try writing a regency or historical romance. Romance is probably the largest, most diverse and most popular of the commercial genres. Some of the best romance writers include Victoria Holt, Judith McNaught, Daphne Du Maurier, Jennifer Greene and Nora Roberts.

**Women's fiction** describes stories which focus on relationships and/or family; one or more strong female protagonists; women triumphing over difficult circumstances; and the experiences of women working together in some way. Sub-genres are usually age-related, such as chick-lit, hen-lit and, more recently, boomer-lit. There is also cross-over with romance.

Women buy more books than men so this is a strong genre, beloved of publishers, and mostly mainstream. Best-selling women's writers include Barbara Taylor Bradford, Anne Rivers Siddons, Judith Krantz, Anne Tyler, and Alice Hoffman.

**Science fiction/fantasy** novels tell stories of imagined worlds in future or parallel time zones with science and technology that may be close to or a million miles from those we know. They are often allegories and discuss contemporary issues from a different perspective. This is a robust genre that goes from strength to strength, and is made ever more popular by big budget films of epic novels from *Harry Potter* to *Lord of the Rings*.

The range of authors in this genre span Ray Bradbury, Arthur C. Clarke, Isaac Asimov, C.S. Lewis, J.K. Rowling and J.R.R. Tolkien.

**Historical fiction,** by definition, tells a story set in the past. That setting is a real historical period, often during an important event of the era. Sometimes the main characters are historical persons (such as Hilary Mantel's *Wolf Hall* trilogy about Thomas Cromwell); in other books they are fictional (eg Bernard Cornwell's *Sharpe* series). Writers of this genre use in depth research combined with language and imagination to present the reality of life, political and social conditions of the time. Period detail and authenticity portrayed through invented eyes make a successful piece of historical fiction.

Sub-genres include historical romance, historical thriller, historical mystery and steampunk (that typically features steam-powered machinery in a 19th century setting with a science fiction element).

**Thriller**, or **Suspense** fiction is different from mystery in that these novels are dominated by physical action and a strong sense of threat to the protagonists. Thrillers are tense, exciting, often sensational stories with fast, skillful plotting and continuous suspense. Often a hero (James Bond, George Smilie) is pitted against an evil villain and the cost of losing the battle would cause national or international disaster. This genre includes espionage, police, courtroom, military and now technological thrillers, among others.

**Horror** continues to be a popular genre with a broad appeal to readers wanting to experience gut-wrenching fright and blood-thirsty action. From a writer's perspective, the intention is to scare readers by exploiting their fears, whether of ghosts, aliens, violence, madness, death or destruction. Stephen King (also writing as Richard Bachman) is the master of the modern genre, following on from the classics of Edgar Allen Poe and Mary Shelley. Very different horror authors include Roald Dahl, Clive Barker, Peter Straub, Dean Koontz, and Anne Rice.

**Young adult** stories are aimed at and about young people aged 12 to 18 (so teenagers, rather than adults), and address the concerns of that age group. YA fiction can be mainstream or fantasy, even historical or science fiction. This is yet another genre where J.K. Rowling's *Harry Potter* novels dominate, and Judy Blume and Louis Sachar have taken over from classic writers like William Golding and J.D. Sallinger.

A new sub genre called **New Adult** fiction has recently surfaced, aimed at 18 to 30-year olds, and stories centre on a young adult's journey into adulthood. These are often coming of age stories and a move from innocence into the more complicated adult world. New adult books can be racier and more violent than young adult books and can also involve a first job, first relationship, first home…

A few other less well known sub-genres, in which you might usefully place your fiction, are: **Adventure fiction** - in which characters are involved in dangerous and/or exhilarating exploits; **Allegory** - which uses symbolism to talk about the human condition; **Black comedy** - humorous stories based on the misfortunes of characters, a sub-genre of **Comedy**, as is **Comedy of manners** - fiction that holds up social attitudes and prejudices to laughter.

**Detective/Police fiction** is a more specific sub-genre of mystery; while **Epistolary fiction** is written as a series of letters exchanged between characters; **Fictional autobiography** purports to be a first-person account of someone's life; and **Fictional biography** tells a tale as if it were a factual life story.

**Picaresque fiction** are (often rambling) stories in which the hero (or antihero) journeys through a series of loosely related episodes; **Parody** is a mocking take-off of a genre style or another author's work; while **Satire** pokes fun at human shortcomings such as arrogance, greed and vanity.

**Swashbucklers** are adventure stories in which the hero accomplishes great feats for noble causes – often in historical settings; the plots of **Travelogues** are centred on a travel or journeys; and **Westerns** are a historical sub-genre set in the pioneering days of wild west America.

**8**

# PLOT DEVELOPMENT
# – CREATING YOUR STORY 'BIBLE'

## Beginning and Ending

You have written a plot overview, developed your characters, understood your setting, explored the theme of your work of fiction, considered the research element and decided what form and genre you will be writing for. The fundamental building blocks are in place – congratulations!

Now we are going to expand your plot, taking the eight sections from the one-page breakdown, and turning each into a full chapter outline (which you may choose to break into more – or fewer – actual chapters when you start writing). Once you have this extended plot outline, the detailed skeleton of your work will have taken shape and the job of writing – adding flesh to those bones – will be so much less daunting.

Some writers claim to skip this stage, to write from instinct and let the plot and their characters develop freely without plans or preconceptions. My guess is that most successful authors who work like this have written many books (not necessarily all published), during which they have internalised the process that we are making explicit. If you are in the early stages of your fiction-writing career, working rigorously through this development approach will stand you in good stead for now, and allow you to make shortcuts in the future.

To recap on the plot outline, we discussed two structural principles for story-telling: the **Three Act** form, breaking narrative into Beginning, Middle and End; and the **Story Arc** which draws the reader through the twists and turns of your plot. We created an eight-point plot overview, of which the first two sections were grouped as 'Beginning', and the last two, 'End'.

You won't be surprised to find that we are going to start by working on Section 1 of the Beginning, which was headed **The Trigger**, but you might not have guessed that, in parallel to this, we are going straight to the final Section 8, **Resolution**.

> 'If I didn't know the ending of a story, I wouldn't begin. I always write my last lines, my last paragraph first, and then I go back and work towards it. I know where I'm going. I know what my goal is. And how I get there is God's grace.'
>
> KATHERINE ANNE PORTER

First, we are going to make use, not of 'God's grace', but the Zeigarnik Effect. In the 1920s, a Russian psychologist called Bluma Zeigarnik noticed, while sitting in a café, that once the waiters opened an order for a table they were able to keep all the details accurately in their minds until the order was completed and paid for – at which point they lost almost all knowledge of it. Psychologists since have noted that this facility can be made use of in task completion: making a small gesture which corresponds to opening an order helps us to focus on, hold in mind complex elements of, and complete a task.

So, let's 'open an order' for your entire plot. In your fiction 'bible', open eight new pages. Head them:

1. **Trigger**

2. **Quest Begins**

3. **Quest Continue**

4. **Reversal 1**

5. **Reversal 2**

6. **Reversal 3**

7. **Climax**

8. **Resolution**

Remember, in the Story Arc, **The Trigger** is the inciting action or event which sets off the entire plot; and **Resolution** is where the last threads are untangled and loose ends tied up.

From your one-page plot outline, take the notes you made on Sections 1 and 8 and transfer them to the first and last of your new pages. You are now going to expand these brief notes into two chapter breakdowns, each between one and two pages long. Create detailed notes about the scenes you will need to set, and complete; the main plot, and however many subplots you intend to have in your story. In Section 1, it is important to carefully frame the inciting event which will set your cast off on their quest; Section 8 should reflect the way this happens when it is resolved.

These two chapters should be mirror images of each other: one way of looking at the beginning and end of a story is to say the first poses a number of questions and the second provides the answers to them. Another is to say that in the first, the author makes the reader a promise; in the last s/he keeps that promise. By the end, the characters' opening positions should be replaced by more mature attitudes produced by the journey they have been on. The 'old world' which you will establish in the opening will be replaced by a 'new world' at the end.

The main plot, involving the main characters, should be started in Section 1 and resolved in Section 8, although it may be that one or more of your sub plots will not appear until later in the story and perhaps finish earlier. There might also be deaths, disappearances and replacements on the journey, so a presence in the Trigger section may be balanced by an absence in Resolution.

What you don't need to know at this moment is what the journey between consists of, but if you don't have a clear idea of the beginning and the ending (although either may be adjusted in the writing), you won't be able to plot the path from one to the other.

## Starting the Journey

Every work of fiction takes its main characters on a journey – known in literature as 'the quest'. Many of the less important characters accompany them on this journey, or embark on their own, different but related quests. Some of the lesser characters may be 'static' – they remain in the same position, in a constant world, with an unchanging attitude throughout the plot – but this tends to make them the least interesting part of your story.

Whether you are writing an epic novel or a very short story, the quest is the essence of fiction and can take almost any form conceivable. The classic form of hero's quest tales are found in ancient mythology: for instance, Jason and the Argonauts go on a hazardous journey to find and bring home the Golden Fleece; Theseus negotiates the seas and a maze to slay the Minotaur and returns with white sails on his ship to herald his success.

Physical journeys into strange lands remain a popular story line for authors from Daniel Defoe to Philip Pullman, but the plot structure of 'the quest' encompasses all fiction, from murder mystery (the quest to find the killer) and romance (the quest for the one true love), to quests for revenge, happiness, truth, justice, self-understanding, health, scientific knowledge and the meaning of life…

However exotic or mundane, literal or metaphorical the quest(s) of your story are, they need to go through well-defined phases to keep your readers engaged. We have worked on outlines for Section 1, **The Trigger**, and skipped straight from there to the final Section 8, **Resolution**. So, now we have in place the 'inciting incident' – the event or action that sets the hero/heroine on their quest – and we know how their story will finish, it's time for them to embark on their journey.

We are going to work on Section 2, **Quest Begins,** and Section 3, **Quest Continues,** of your chapter breakdown. From your one-page plot outline, take the notes you made on Sections 2 and 3 and transfer them to the new pages for these sections you have opened and headed. As with Sections 1 and 8, you are now going to expand these into two chapter breakdowns, each between one and two pages long.

This part of a novel can be something of a danger zone. The interest and excitement of the opening, meeting new characters and the shock of the inciting incident grabs a reader's interest. Later, the characters' development and the twists and turns of the plot will keep the reader wanting to get to the end of your story. But right now, maintaining that interest as you set up and begin the quest is challenging, so consider which of these devices may help you do that as you embark on your story.

Is the main character reluctant to take on the quest? Is it frightening, dangerous or pushes them out of their comfort zone? In what way can you engage the reader in their difficult decision to take the first step? Does another character, or a new piece of information or action, provide an added incentive? Alternatively, is the hero(ine) keen to get started, but circumstances or other characters are against them? If so, what are the reasons – do we suspect foul play at this point, ulterior motives of others for derailing the quest? In either scenario, maintaining an element of mystery about the difficulty of starting the quest will keep the reader wanting to know why, whether it will actually happen or how it will affect the outcome.

Remember, as you set up the quest, to keep asking, but not yet answering, for the reader, the questions: *Who? What? Why? When? Where? How?*

Following the initial Trigger section, your job in Section 2 is to ensure the reader believes in the vital importance that the quest should happen, is drawn in further by the possibility that it might not, but reassured at the end of the **Quest Begins** section, that the protagonist is on their way.

In Section 3, the **Quest Continues,** your plot moves into a new phase: the set up of the main story is done, the reader has set off on the journey with the main characters. This, then, can be an ideal time to introduce a new element: a fresh or simmering sub plot that counterpoints the main plot with a parallel or opposite quest; or threatens to undermine the protagonists now or at some later point in the story. Alternatively, or additionally, a new, positive character could come into play (an ongoing confidant or supporter – a Dr Watson or Man Friday) to add richness and subtlety to The Quest, or new skills or perspectives to help achieve it.

For Sections 2 and 3, create detailed notes about the scenes you will need to set, snatches of dialogue, and remember to set up hints and clues, the significance of which the reader will not find out till later. Keep in mind the Resolution you have already outlined and make sure that everything you set up in Sections 2 and 3 can be resolved in the way you have defined (although adjustments to the ending can be made at any time).

Look back, too, over what you have written about your plot overview, characters' development, your story's setting and theme, and make sure your chapter breakdowns stay consistent with these. Doing this will also remind you how much you have achieved so far, and will make the writing, when you begin, much easier and more enjoyable.

## Reversals

We are getting deeper into the plotting of your work of fiction. Within the Three Act form, we've completed The Beginning, started The Middle and have the final part of The End sorted out. This leaves us with the meaty part of the plot to fill out: the remaining sections of The Middle, or Second Act, where it develops through a series of complications and obstacles – **Reversals** – each leading to a crisis. Though the initial crises are temporarily resolved, they collectively and inevitably lead to an ultimate crisis at the third reversal...

The eight-part structure, with three sets of **Reversals,** is geared towards a novel-length work of fiction – typically around 80,000 words (a publisher's ideal length). You won't be able to fit this many into a micro-story or probably a short story, either of which might only need one reversal to make the plot work; in a novelette or novella, two reversals could be plenty, while if you are writing a novel of epic proportions, you may need to extend the Middle section with additional reversals.

From this point on, having set your main characters off on their Quest, you can imagine your story arc as a graph: as the storyline progresses, there is an overall rising of tension, with an upward spike at each reversal, followed by small dips as the first two are resolved. The tension spike of each reversal is higher than the last, with the third providing a high point before **The Climax**.

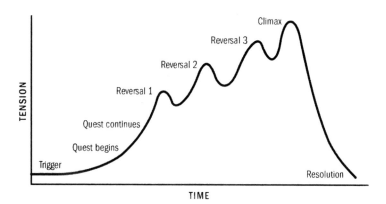

You may find a personal structural image will help you manage your plotting. When I was writing *Blood and Water*, I visualised the detective story as an old-fashioned roller coaster where each new piece of information cranked the train further towards the summit and, once everything was in place, the train gained its own momentum and flew ever faster downhill round the twists and turns until the truth had unraveled. But the dual time-scheme of *Kindred Spirits* looked to me like the creation of an elaborate hairstyle, where many strands had to be introduced and woven in evenly from different sides, curls pinned here and ends tucked in there, sometimes a little bit of faking it, to create a complex but satisfying reading experience.

Once again, take the notes you made on Sections 4, 5 and 6 from your one-page plot outline, and transfer them to the new pages for these sections you have opened and headed, to expand them into chapter breakdowns of between one and two pages long. If you are running one or more subplots, it might help you to keep track of each one separately, in horizontal layers on your pages, which may mean these three section outlines are longer than two pages. Try to create little sub-spikes in the story arc just before or after those of your main plot. It will become confusing if all your reversals happen together - though at the final reversal, this can produce a powerful crisis point.

A couple of tips to keep on track with main plot and sub-plot reversals include:

1. Run a timeline through Sections 3, 4 and 5 especially. Important things to track are when important events occur (including before your story opens), when people meet each other, and who knows what when. You don't want characters acting on information they don't yet know, talking about people who haven't entered the story yet, or somehow being unaware of important events they should know about.

2.  If your story is dependent on setting, or where and
    how things happen geographically, draw a map or
    building plan and make sure characters are in the
    right place at the right time, that their journeys
    are timed right and even that they can actually
    see events they are supposed to have witnessed.

What might your **Reversals** consist of? The second
act is predominantly about your characters' emotional journey and is both the most fun and the
most challenging part of a story to create. The key to
rising tension and the reader being gripped by the
story is conflict – both external, possibly physical,
and emotional inner conflict. Try to advance both
inner and outer struggles simultaneously; each external conflict should relate to a character's internal
conflict, teaching them a life lesson or giving them
the option to change. Keep raising the stakes.

 Include reversals of fortune and unexpected turns of
events: surprise your reader with both the actions of
the main characters and the events surrounding them,
but make sure you have developed credible reasons
and motives, even if you haven't told the reader of
them in advance. Classic journey plots include reversals such as Monsters, Temptations, Deadly Oppo-
sites, Dream to Nightmare, Capture and Escape, Journey to the Underworld, Arrival and Frustration, Giv-

ing Up, and Final Ordeals. Have fun coming up with contemporary versions of these; they work!

Your last reversal must be where tension, perhaps danger, and the stakes are highest before the **Climax**. During this moment, the hero/ine/s draw upon the new strengths or lessons they've learned in order to take action, in anticipation of bringing the story to a conclusion.

## The Climax

All you have left to complete now, in the plot outline of your novel or short story, is the beginning of the end: Part 7 of the eight-part structure we outlined at the start.

**The Climax** comes at the end of the series of Reversals that your characters have faced, which have created the central action of the story.

We are now at the crucial point to which the plot and any sub-plots have been leading and, if all the work you have done on The Beginning and The Middle have followed the plan, this section should more or less write itself – and fit neatly before Section 8, the final part of The End which you have already elucidated.

Whatever your genre or story, its climax must be gripping, tense, full of suspense and yet inevitable, given the trajectory of the action and the development of the characters. The reader must expect some of what is coming, but be desperate to know how it will happen and which way the outcome will go. Whether it involves a declaration of love, a pitched battle, a race against time to stop the murderer or a personal revelation, a fictional climax is best played out as a dramatic set piece of choreographed action which involves all the facets of your novel.

The Characters are, of course, primary. Your hero/ine/s have been on a learning curve throughout the story: with each reversal they will either have been knocked back or (more usually) developed in strength and integrity. The climax is the final test in which they prove themselves (unless you are writing a tragedy), take control, use their new found knowledge and abilities for the best and finally turn around their circumstances. In order for it to matter to the reader, the confrontation of the climax must be a matter of literal or metaphorical life or death to the characters.

The action of this section will require a build-up, where the sequence of events develops, a crucial decision is made by the main character(s) to act, followed by the confrontation itself. This is where your characters' internal transformation intersects with the outer plot that has made that transformation possible. Their moment of truth or revelation determines their course of action in the climax.

The Setting is also central to the climax. If the plot journey has been a physical or geographical one, your characters will have moved from the world in which they started their journey to the place of their new order. Part of their Quest may have been to discover or travel to a new environment, whether it's a redecorated apartment, a different country or the conquering of another planet. The climax might also take the heroes into enemy or alien territory and their reaction to the setting will affect the action and outcome.

Whether the climactic setting is menacing or inspiring, reflects or counterpoints the characters' emotions, or provides a dramatic backdrop through weather or scenery, make sure you use it to the full in developing the action and drawing the reader through the intensity of your story's climax. Remember the notes you made on period, society, ethos and geography; reflect on how they have changed throughout your story, or remained static but changed the people within them. Make reference to them in your climax scenes, to draw all the threads of your story into a high point of descriptive writing.

Refer back, too, to the Themes you developed early on in your fiction 'bible'. These should have been informing your plot development and will come to the fore in the climax scenes. To draw out your themes initially, you asked some questions, including: what does the reader know at the end of this story that they didn't know at the beginning; and what do the characters learn as a result of their journey in this story? This is the time when these questions must be answered: the climax is the fulfilment of the promise you made to your readers when you invited them into your book.

Checking in with the themes you set out to address at the start will also help you bring the story to a close which is satisfactory to you, the characters and the reader. If, like me, you were always told at school to 'answer the question' posed in the essay title and not digress, you can use your themes in a similar way. If you find your climactic action getting untidy or losing focus, ask yourself how it relates to your key themes and, if it doesn't, edit it out.

Your climax may build and peak over several linked events. To maximise the drama, visualise them as scenes in a movie and use all your senses – sight, sound, smell, taste and touch, as well as emotion – to describe them. Many novelists take this opportunity to create a dramatic set piece to bring all the characters together: a party, a public event, a battle, a crime scene. These need to be carefully plotted to weave different strands together, building tension, danger and expectation.

Remember, though, that not everything has to be explained in the climax. Crime fiction, for example, often uses the climax scenes to mislead the reader one last time. The police work out where the crime is to be committed, surround the murderer and her victim; the detective goes in to prevent the killing, but a shot is fired and a scream heard. A tense climax – but the author may wait till the Resolution to tell the reader who was actually killed and by whom, and clarify the remaining unexplained pieces of information that brought the plot to its climactic point.

As you expand the notes you made on Section 7 from your one-page plot outline into a one-to-two page chapter breakdown, take the time to plot your climax with great care and attention to detail. Think through the timing of each piece of action, the specific locations, the emotions and motivation of each character, the thematic significance of all aspects.

Now your story 'bible' is complete, we'll get started on the real writing process.

# PART TWO

# WRITING

# 9

# FINDING YOUR VOICE

Now all the preparation for your work of fiction is done, you are ready to start writing.

The day you truly enter the alternative world that you will inhabit for the next few weeks, months or even years, is an exciting moment – and sometimes a scary one. At least you are not facing a blank page or screen: you have your completed story 'bible', with its plot overview and section breakdowns, character descriptions, setting and theme. Your hard work will have paid off, in that you know where your story will start and end, as well as most of the twists and turns along the way.

To keep yourself focused, pin a copy of your one-page plot outline somewhere in view of your desk and open the chapter breakdown of Section 1 outlining your Beginning. You could copy these pages and use them as a template from which to expand your narrative, section by section.

If you find it hard to get started, remember that at this point you don't have to write something brilliant – or even something good; you just have to write *something*. This is only your first draft; later it can be polished, revised or cut entirely.

> **'Get it down, take chances. It may be bad, but it's the only way you can do anything good.'**
> **WILLIAM FAULKNER**

Many authors have advised that once you have finished a book you should go back to the start and ruthlessly cut your original opening, up to the point at which, it will now be clear, the action really starts. The paragraphs, or even chapters, with which you initially felt your way into the story, can often simply be dispensed with. So don't feel too attached to what you write today; it is a beginning, and an important first step in your story, but it might not survive through to the end.

Your first job when you start a new piece of fiction is to find your writing voice and to do that you may have to experiment a bit. The first decision to be made is about the narrative point of view you are going to take – in other words, who is going to be telling your story? There are a number of tried and tested options.

A **First-person view** is where your story is narrated by one of your characters using the first person pronoun ('I...'). All of the action is relayed from his or her point of view and nothing can be told (unless reported to your narrator by another character or device) without this person having witnessed it. This means that the story is also interpreted through your main character's understanding, and gives you the opportunity for her or his incomplete knowledge and misunderstandings to be a key part of the plot development.

**First-person narrative** is usually, but not always, written from the main protagonist's point of view; it can also come from someone close to the main char-acter(s), an observer of the action or someone dis-covering events that happened earlier. It allows you to convey their internal thoughts and feelings di-rectly to the reader and to develop their complexity. When you write as a first person narrator, your style will be the voice of the character.

**Alternating first-person view** is another choice you could make for your narrative voice(s). If you have two, or more, characters who are key to the action, you might switch between their viewpoints, writing as 'I...' for each of them in turn. You need to find a way of clearly differentiating between these characters' voices for the reader, in terms of writing style and point of view, possibly even typographically or heading their individual sections with the characters' names. This split narrative point of view works particularly well if your plot takes place in different times or places and gives you the chance to develop writing styles from both genders, other eras and opposing perspectives.

**Third-person view**, where your narrator is an unspecified person or being, outside the action, and therefore refers to all the characters as 'he', 'she' or 'they', provides you as an author with the most flexibility and is the most commonly used narrative mode in fiction.

The **third-person narrator** can be an 'objective' voice, describing the action but not the thoughts or feelings of any characters from the inside (which doesn't stop the characters talking about their own feelings to each other). Or you can write 'subjective' third-person narration, which is privy either to one, some or all of the characters' inner lives. A third-person narrator can also be omniscient, and have access to all events, times, people and places; or they can be limited to having full knowledge from one character's point of view, but not from the others (making this closer to first-person narration).

Be careful, if you choose a third-person omniscient narrator, not to commit the sin of 'head-hopping' – by which I mean confusing the reader by too frequently jumping between characters' points of view. For instance, it rarely works to give the reader the thoughts of more than one character in a single paragraph, or to intersperse dialogue between two or more characters with all their individual feelings and responses to each other. Unless you are a very experienced writer, you will do better to stick with one character's point of view in any single scene, and clearly delineate when a new character becomes the focus.

**Alternating third-person view** involves the narrator describing the characters from the outside ('he...', 'she...'), but only having intimate knowledge of one at a time, so telling the story from alternate characters' points of view whilst remaining an exterior entity. In this case, you can choose either to maintain a single, objective narrator's voice for describing all the characters, or the voice can change to reflect the individual styles of each character, as the narrator focuses on them.

Even if you have already decided on the narrator view for your novel or short story, get your writing started with a few experiments from different viewpoints. Try out two or three of the characters as possible narrators – in first-person and third-person voices – and test some different styles for a limited or omniscient narrator. They might be naïve or cynical; take a humorous or dark approach. Do they speak informally to the reader, or do they have a literary turn of phrase? Don't commit yourself to a voice until you feel comfortable about taking it right through your story.

# 10

# HOOKING YOUR READER

Having tried out some different voices and points of view, you will have decided on the narrative style for your work of fiction. Although you may want to just get writing, to start the words flowing and your story moving, you will need to carefully craft – if not now, then later – the opening lines of your story.

> **"There's one thing I'm sure about. An opening line should invite the reader to begin the story. It should say: Listen. Come in here. You want to know about this."**
>
> STEPHEN KING

The first few sentences, or paragraphs, are crucial to getting the reader's involvement. If they don't invest emotionally in the story now, you may lose them at some point along the journey. Imagine a potential reader opening the first page in a book-shop or library, or checking the 'Look Inside' function online and deciding whether or not to buy. If you have sent your manuscript to an agent, editor or publisher, their decision on whether to read on or pass it up is likely to be taken here. This is your chance to pique their interest, make them want to read on and continue through to the very end.

The *do*s and *don'ts* to writing a great opening to your story are known as **hooks** – as in getting your reader hooked.

'A good writer should draw the reader in by starting in the middle of the story with a hook, then go back and fill in what happened before the hook. Once you have the reader hooked, you can write whatever you want as you slowly reel them in.'

ROLAND SMITH

- **Do – start in the middle of some action.** Parachute your reader into something exciting, intriguing or extraordinary; the story is already happening as they start reading and they are drawn straight in.

- **Don't – start with the back story**. It's a mistake to think you need to explain who people are and why they are there before you can get on with the action. On the contrary, the best fiction writing weaves information in with action, dialogue and character development throughout the plot.

- **Do – get the reader asking questions.** Your first few sentences should make the reader want to know: What is going on? Who is this person/people? How and Why did they get here? And crucially, What is going to happen to them?

- **Don't – spoon feed your reader.** Part of the pleasure of reading fiction is building up your own picture from the clues and information that the writer carefully positions throughout the narrative.

- **Do – provide some context.** Hint at the setting, situation and, if appropriate, historical period; suggest that whatever the current position, things are going to change.

- **Don't – make the opening so bizarre** that readers can't make any sense of it or identify with the character(s) early on.

Here are three examples of strong openings which hook the reader by sticking to these rules. They are from the winning entries in the Rethink Press New Novels 2012 Competition, and successfully hooked the judges to nominate them.

A January morning. Terrible cold, terrible hunger. The constants. At the back of those constants, another. Her. Sarah. Far away, eight hundred miles to the south. I opened my eyes and there, across the cabin, her husband, Edward, wrapping rags of blanket around his legs, tying them on with twine from our old parcels. Edward, who had hardly been home a month before planning to leave again.

James Ferron Anderson opens *The River and The Sea,* a literary tale of romance and adventure, in a very few words  that set us in a place and situation we recognise as dire, though we don't know why, and introduces us to a romantic triangle – a husband, an absent wife and a narrator who is in love with her. The reader immediately wants to know how those relationships came about, why the two men are separated from 'her', and what cruel environment has brought them to this physical deprivation.

By contrast, Angela Lawrence's *Rumour,* a fictionalised account of real life incidents which took place at the start of World War 1, intrigues the reader by opening with a much more specific context:

## Sunday June 28 1914

The day Archduke Ferdinand and his wife were assassinated in Sarajevo, being a Sunday, William Smith and his wife Alma went to church.

The student's bullets found their mark at about the time they were dismissing their Sunday School classes. And by the time they rose from their pew at the end of Evensong the Archduke and his beloved Sophie had been dead for many hours.

Their corpses by now cold and rigid, their reputations, and the significance of their sudden end, subject to hasty dissection by journalists for the following day's newspapers.

While the lives of one devoted couple, celebrating their wedding anniversary on a state visit to Bosnia, had been extinguished in the flash of a gunman's eye, the modest existence of another passed wholly unremarkably in a Suffolk village.

As well as instant period context, the author contrasts the well known characters and incident which gave rise to the First World War, with a 'modest' Sunday School-teaching couple in a Suffolk village. By doing this the author makes it clear that a link between them will be established, but leaves us guessing as to how. Who, we wonder, are William and Alma Smith and what will their story be? Clearly their lives are going to change.

The Runner Up in the competition was a college campus murder mystery called *Dead Letter Day* by Keri Beevis.

> He had known from the beginning that they would come for him eventually and in a way he guessed he was lucky that it had taken them so long to find him.
>
> Almost eight years. Seven years, ten months and twenty-seven days, if you wanted to be exact.
>
> He knew, of course, because he had counted those days in thick black marker pen on the white emulsion wall, each one that had passed denoted with a red circle, there in plain view for anyone who entered the room to see.
>
> Of course nobody ever had seen. But that was the beauty of hiding; no one was supposed to know where you were.

This opening introduces the murderer, we assume, and implies an imminent change in his circumstances – the hiding he has been in for almost eight years. In the nature of the crime thriller genre, the reader puts together the clues, along with the detective, to reach an unexpected but satisfying conclusion, so the opening must start that process. The beginning of *Dead Letter Day* raises all the questions that must be answered by the end: what crimes have been committed; by whom; who is the criminal and how will s/he be discovered? It does so without either giving away any of the back story, or making what is clearly a bizarre situation too alienating to engage with.

Whether you spend time fashioning your story's opening now, or come back at the end to polish it, check out other examples of your chosen genre and bear in mind the *Dos* and *Don'ts* of hooking the reader.

# 11

## SHOW AND TELL

You might have crafted a killer opening to your story, or you may have decided to come back and polish it after you've got to the end. Either way, you know that hooking your reader at the start depends on not giving too much away at once. That continues to hold true throughout your writing.

'Show, don't tell,' is a piece of advice frequently given to new fiction writers, and there is a lot of value in taking this on board. What it means is that, instead of summarising action and telling your reader what is happening, you demonstrate and illustrate, allowing your reader to draw their own conclusions and make the links that draw them through the story under their own steam. For example, an author could tell you that a character was a controlling and mean-spirited man. As a reader you would have to accept this, but not be able engage your critical faculties in coming to this decision.

In *Birdsong*, Sebastian Faulks writes:

'Do you drink wine?' said Azaire, holding a bottle over Stephen's glass.

'Thank you.'

Azaire poured out an inch or two for Stephen and for his wife, before returning the bottle to its place.

From this, and further dialogue and details in the scene, the reader gains the pleasure of creating their own picture of Azaire and his character without Faulks ever having told us this in so many words.

To 'show' as opposed to 'telling' your story means that you need to break down much of the action in terms of scenes, similar to a screenplay. So, as you come to each chapter outline in your fiction 'bible', decide what scenes you need to 'show' in order to move the plot along. As you write each scene, remember to use all your senses in describing what is going on: not just what you (and the characters) can see, but what is heard, felt, smelled, touched and experienced.

Consider this sentence:

He went to bed late, hoping his wife would be asleep so he would not have to talk to her, but she was not.

This gives a reader the same factual information as Elizabeth Jane Howard does in the following passage from *The Light Years*, but lacks the visual, sensory and emotional power – as well as additional, subtle knowledge we gain about the characters – that she includes by 'showing' the scene:

> He opened the bedroom door hoping that Zoe would be asleep. She wasn't, of course. She was sitting up in bed, her bedjacket on her shoulders, doing nothing, waiting for him. He fumbled with his tie and had dropped it on top of his chest of drawers before she said, 'You've been a long time.' Her voice had the controlled quality that he had learned to dread.

'Showing' as opposed to 'telling' also helps you to avoid the type of narration that is often called 'And then, and then...'. This is when an author takes the reader through the plot via a series of events, one after the other, frequently not discriminating between the interesting/important elements of the story and those which link them but have no intrinsic significance to the theme or plot. The opposite to 'And then, and then...' writing is known as the 'Why? Because' style. In other words, the choice of scenes, description etc, is governed by motive, character development and interaction.

You will notice, however, from the above excerpts and my paraphrases of them that the 'told' version is much shorter than the 'shown' scene. And, of course, a novel or short story are not the same as a screenplay for the very reason that, unlike a script, they include description, linkage, exposition and the interior thought processes of the characters. So is there a place in good fiction writing for 'telling'?

The answer, of course, is yes. Excellent narrative combines a majority (usually) of 'showing' and some strategic 'telling' to link scenes, provide contrast in pace and content, and provide information quickly and which can't always be given in another way.

When you are deciding which are the key scenes to 'show' in each section of your story, make sure that they are essential to the development of your plot, relate strongly to your theme and demonstrate character development.

To link your key scenes and provide a change of tempo and style, use 'telling' segments to get across information and get through less crucial events. The idea is to find a good balance of 'telling' versus 'showing', summary versus action.

One tip is not to go into detail about, or develop dialogue for, characters who are unimportant or not going to reappear in the story. For example, an interchange with a receptionist when checking into a hotel is best summarised rather than 'shown', although a few specifics, as opposed to generalities, when describing the hotel foyer or the receptionist will always give the reader an additional picture to add into the rich mix of your story.

# **12**

# **WRITING DIALOGUE**

A large part of 'showing', as opposed to 'telling' your story is about creating scenes in which the characters interact – and interaction means dialogue.

> **'[A]lways get to the dialogue as soon as possible. I always feel the thing to go for is speed. Nothing puts the reader off more than a big slab of prose at the start.'**
>
> P.G. WODEHOUSE

Fiction dialogue has to appear realistic, but, paradoxically, if the reader is to believe in it, cannot be genuinely life-like. If you pasted into your novel a slab of real-life conversation, it would be unfocused, long-winded, boring and – strangely – would appear unnatural. If you've ever tried to read verbatim transcripts of interviews, you'll know how hard they are to plough through. Readers don't want to see in print the ums and ers, pauses, digressions and waffling that everyday chat consists of.

As a fiction writer, you need to give readers the essence of what your characters are communicating with the flavour of verisimilitude. So how do you do that?

First you need to find the individual voice of each character – especially your main characters – in your head. Don't try to write their dialogue until you can hear them speak; recognise the pitch and tone of their voice, their accent and intonation; understand the way their speech reflects their thought processes; and the verbal tics that are uniquely theirs.

If a character doesn't come easily to you, the simplest way to find their voice is to base it on that of someone you know well, whether personally or from the media. Find someone whose distinctive style of speaking is easy for you to reproduce in your head and apply to your character's dialogue. As you keep writing, the character will come to life and subsume the style of your original model until you don't need to refer back to them.

Each character in your story – even the minor ones – should have an individual style of speaking. The test of this is for someone to be able to read a page of dialogue between two or more of your characters and always know, without referring to the tags ('x said', 'y replied'), which of them is speaking. A sure-fire way to lose a reader's interest is to have all your characters talking in the same style, despite their different ages, backgrounds, education, gender, etc.

One shortcut to identifying a character through dialogue is to give them a couple of verbal habits – though subtlety is the key here. For example, an older man could always call other men 'old chap' and women 'my dear'; a teenager might punctuate their speech with 'like' and 'you know'; an academic could habitually use longer words where a short one would do; a hesitant woman might regularly start sentences with, 'Well, ...'. Using such words or phrases initially as an identity tag will help you define a character's verbal style, and you might later be able to go back and remove the more obvious ones.

If a character speaks with an accent of any kind, do *not* try to write it phonetically. Everyone speaks with an accent of one kind or another, whether we consider it 'received English' or something else. Your readers themselves may come from any part of your country, or the world, and might find it offensive for their own manner of speech to be written in a different way to what you, the writer, consider 'normal' English. The best way to indicate national, regional, age- or class-based accents is in the style and tone of the language along with a few judiciously placed words (spelled correctly) or phrases which are natural to and typical of your character's accent. Along with the context you give them, the reader will 'get' what you intend and supply the appropriate accent as they read.

In general, when you are writing dialogue, use contractions ('don't', 'he's', 'shouldn't'), as almost everyone does in real speech, unless the character is very formal and not to do so becomes their verbal tic. Allow characters to speak in verbless phrases and incomplete sentences in a way that sounds authentic, and contrasts (probably) with your narrative style. The occasional 'um' or 'er' can sound natural, but a life-like amount would become tedious. Similarly, allow characters to interrupt and cut across each other occasionally, but not as much as people really do or your dialogue will become impossible to follow.

In using dialogue to 'show' your story, make sure that every exchange contains something that either furthers the plot or adds to character development and ties into one or more of your themes. Don't use dialogue to give the reader information or back story in an obvious way, unless one character is telling another who doesn't already know and needs to know this information.

Use dialogue judiciously. Readers don't want or need to be shown an entire conversation, including exchanges such as:

'Pass the salt.'

'There it is.'

'Thank you. And the pepper, please.'

Summarise between significant pieces of dialogue – readers are quite capable of understanding 'jump cuts'. Remember to keep your dialogue interspersed with action and description. People continue to eat, walk, drive, wash up, etc, while they are speaking and you need to keep 'showing' this.

There are grammatical rules for writing dialogue. Speech should be enclosed in inverted commas (single or double – but single is most common these days), which contain the punctuation related to the dialogue. Start a new line each time a different person starts to speak and, if it is followed by action by the same character, continue this in the same paragraph. Some publishers indent new lines of dialogue in typeset, but it's easier for editors and typesetters if authors do *not* indent new lines of dialogue in a manuscript.

If you insert a tag ('he said') after a sentence of dialogue, the dialogue sentence within the quotation marks ends with a comma, and the full stop/period is postponed until the end of the tag:

'I would be happy to recommend you a very good hotel,' said the taxi driver.

If you insert a tag into the middle of a sentence of dialogue, this is how the punctuation should go:

'I would be happy,' said the taxi driver, 'to recommend you a very good hotel.'

Be sparing with tags; if your dialogue is well written for individual characters, you shouldn't need to say who is speaking after every sentence. Try to refrain from using tags to 'tell' – as in:

'That's awfully good news,' Eleanor shouted excitedly.

The context and the dialogue itself should tell a reader that Eleanor is speaking loudly and with excitement, but you should usually be able to find a verb that subsumes the adjective, such as '…Eleanor yelled', or '…Eleanor exclaimed'.

Some experts say the only verb that should be used in a tag is 'said' and never with an adverb; that seems to me to be unnecessarily restrictive, but less is usually more.

# 13

# STRUCTURING A SENTENCE (PLUS PUNCTUATION)

Whether you are 'showing', 'telling' or composing dialogue, your writing should communicate your meaning to the reader with maximum ease and clarity.

'Be kind to your reader,' was one of the best pieces of advice once given to me by an editor. By this, she meant that making prose simple to understand and easy to follow (however complex the action or ideas) for readers is the best way to keep them engaged in your story.

To do this, it's essential to write grammatically and use punctuation correctly – not for the sake of sticking to rules, but because grammar and punctuation are tools of good communication. They provide a window through which the reader 'sees' your scenes: well-written narrative gives the reader such a clear view that they are not even aware of the glass through which they are looking; mis-punctuated writing with poor grammatical construction is like a dirty window that the reader is constantly distracted by, and through which they peer with difficulty in order to 'see' what's going on.

> **'A sentence should be read as if its author, had he held a plough instead of a pen, could have drawn a furrow deep and straight to the end.'**
>
> HENRY DAVID THOREAU

Let's go back to basics.

**The sentence** is the fundamental building block of prose writing. A sentence can be short or long, but its essential components are:

- to start with a *capital letter*

- to end with a *full stop/period*, and

- to contain a *subject and verb* (the subject is a noun or pronoun who/that carries out the verb)

'I go.' or 'I am.' are perhaps the shortest possible, if not the most elegant, sentences in the English language.

*The house was falling down.*

*War had started.*

*Amy cooked the breakfast.* (This last has an object, the breakfast, as well as a subject.)

These are all complete, grammatical **simple sentences**. They comprise a single, independent clause.

**Imperative sentences**, such as exclamations (*Hello!*), commands (*Get moving!*), and requests (*Please sit down.*), are the only exceptions to the subject/verb sentence rule – though they imply both: *I bid you hello; Would you get moving; Will you please sit down.*

**Simple sentences,** like all these above, need no further punctuation. They are ideal for punchy statements, brusque dialogue and giving a staccato feel to quick action sequences. But your readers would quickly tire of an entire story written like this; with more complex sentence structures comes the greater need to punctuate carefully for sense and readability.

**Compound Sentences** are easy enough: they are essentially two related, simple sentences stuck together with a conjunction, such as 'and', 'but', 'or', 'because', 'although', etcetera.

*Amy cooked the breakfast although war had started.*

This compound sentence, composed of two independent clauses (which could each be a stand-alone sentence), doesn't require any internal punctuation. If, though, you add a third clause –

*Amy cooked the breakfast, although war had started and the house was falling down.*

– adding a comma after the main clause makes it easier for the reader to comprehend.

As a general rule (though there are exceptions, one of which is the Oxford comma), do *not* put a comma before an 'and'; always put a comma before 'but'.

To join two related clauses/sentences *without* a conjunction – and so create a more enigmatic sentence – use a **semi-colon**.

*Amy cooked the breakfast; the war had started and the house was falling down.*

(The context in which you have placed this compound sentence should show the reader that these three clauses are related!)

It is incorrect to use a semi-colon with a conjunction, so you would *not* write: *Amy cooked the breakfast; although the war had started.*

**Compound sentences** are useful for connecting facts and good to mix into your narrative style, but you need more variation than simple and compound sentences to express more involved ideas and situations.

**Complex Sentences** are the next step up the prose ladder and the most dynamic and interesting kind of sentence – to read and to write. The most basic complex sentence consists of a main clause and a dependent clause. The main clause can stand alone, but dependent clauses on their own turn into mere fragments.

*Amy, ignoring the fact that the house was falling down, cooked the breakfast.*

Here, *Amy cooked the breakfast* is the main clause, while *ignoring the fact that the house was falling down* is the sub-clause (and doesn't stand alone).

The key to punctuating complex sentences is knowing where to place the commas. This is *not* – as you may have been taught in school – about inserting a comma where you would pause when speaking. It *is* about separating the sub-clause(s) from the main clause. The sub-clause can come at the start or end of a complex sentence; in either case it only needs one comma to separate it off:

*Ignoring the fact that the house was falling down,* Amy cooked the breakfast.

Amy cooked the breakfast, *ignoring the fact that the house was falling down.*

If you place the sub-clause in the middle of the sentence, though, it must be separated by a comma on both sides:

Amy, *ignoring the fact that the house was falling down,* cooked the breakfast.

Too often, writers omit one of the commas around a central sub-clause, making a sentence hard, if not nonsensical, to read. I would rather see no commas at all than only one around a sub-clause.

Commas should be used in the same way to separate conjunctions: *However,* war had started. War had started, *however.* War, *however,* had started.

At the peak of sentence complexity sits the **Complex-compound sentence**. As you may have guessed, this is a combination of compound and complex sentences. They have two or more main clauses, at least one dependent clause, and often need careful use of the full range of punctuation marks to make sense.

To engage and stimulate your reader's imagination, use a variety of sentence structures in your narrative. You can get the most information across and develop more detailed ideas using complex or complex-compound sentences, but simple and compound sentences are good for straightforward facts, punchy dialogue and fast-moving action.

# 14

# BUILDING A PARAGRAPH
# (AND MORE PUNCTUATION)

Having talked about different kinds of sentence structure, and how to punctuate a sentence, we are now going to look at combining sentences to form paragraphs – and a little more punctuation.

If sentences are the building blocks of prose writing, paragraphs are the panels, doors and windows in the walls of your narrative edifice.

## So, what is a paragraph?

A paragraph is a group of one or more sentences, separated from other paragraphs by starting on a new line and finishing at the end of a final sentence, often in mid-line. Like a sentence, therefore, a paragraph can end with a full stop/period, question or exclamation mark, closed inverted commas, a dash or ellipsis (three – exactly – dots)…

(It could also finish with a closing bracket, but brackets rarely have a place in fiction writing.)

In a printed fiction book, paragraphs are typically indented on the first line (except at the start of a chapter or section), have 'trailing spaces' after the end of the last sentence (ie, the last line is not justified to the right), but are not separated from the paragraph above or below by a line space.

When formatting paragraphs in your manuscript, however, bear in mind that, for technical reasons, most editors and publishers prefer authors *not* to indent the first line of a paragraph (though if you do indent, use the tab key and not the space bar); and to insert a line space between paragraphs.

## What are paragraphs for?

Paragraphs have a physical purpose: they act as a visual break for readers, separating the text into distinct and variable-sized blocks, which help a reader keep their place on the page and also within the action of the story. Pages of solid text, or very long paragraphs, are intimidating, tiring to read and don't draw the eye forwards through the story; too many short paragraphs, though, can make for a jerky and disrupted reading experience.

Just as sentences of differing lengths create changing rhythms for your narrative, so do varying-sized paragraphs. Longer paragraphs usually indicate extended action, detailed description or complex thought processes, so the story becomes slower and more measured as readers work their way through them.

Shorter paragraphs happen around quick exchanges of dialogue, rapid action and the introduction of vital information. An occasional paragraph of a single sentence, or even one word, whether dialogue or narrative, can have a more immediate and powerful effect than several longer paragraphs. They can be used to shock the reader or to make a sharp or sudden point, but should be used sparingly so as not to dissipate their potency.

A good mix of paragraphs of different lengths keeps the reader engaged and varies the speed and tone of plot development. Look at this section and see where your eye is attracted to short, punchy paragraphs in the first instance and how, while you are reading longer ones, you are drawn in into more complex ideas and concepts.

## When should you start a new paragraph?

1. **When you are writing dialogue**. Every time a new character starts to speak, their dialogue should start on a new line and create an individual paragraph. (The word *paragraph* comes from the Greek word *paragraphos* – *para* 'beside' and *graphein* 'to write' – meaning a marginal note used to indicate a change of speaker in drama.) While a single character continues to speak, even if there is action, internal thought or description alternating with their dialogue, it can all stay within one paragraph. As soon as new person starts to speak, their dialogue begins on a new line and paragraph.

2. **When one piece of action, narration or thought finishes**, the new subject matter should start with a new paragraph. If you are covering a protracted event or exposition, use an introductory paragraph; an ending, or summary, paragraph; and as many paragraphs as you need to delineate the stages between.

3. **When the focus of your narrative changes from one character to another** – especially if you are changing from one person's point of view to someone else's – begin a new paragraph.

4.  **When none of the above apply and you are in the middle of a long section**, but you need to give your reader some incentives to get through it. In the same way as you punctuate a sentence to make it easy for your reader to understand, break up your prose into logical paragraphs, manageable bites, to give flow and structure to your story, and visual variation on the page.

## How do you structure a paragraph?

If you think of a paragraph as a frame for a certain amount of information, how to give it the right shape and form becomes clearer. Each paragraph is acting as a boundary for the related items within it. In descriptive writing, it can open with an introductory sentence, followed by others that expand on the opening point, and close with a sentence which sums up or completes the point. Just as a picture frame should be the best size and shape to display the painting it contains, so a paragraph should neatly contain the chunk of information being conveyed to the reader.

*Read the above paragraph again and note how it is shaped in this way.*

A dialogue paragraph will start with a character's first sentence of speech. They may continue speaking throughout the paragraph; you may break it up to tag the dialogue, to describe theirs, or another character's, internal or external responses before adding more dialogue; or intersperse their dialogue with action. In most cases, the dialogue paragraph naturally ends when another character starts to speak, but if one character talks at length, you may need to divide their speech into subject- or emotion-related paragraphs.

## How to order paragraphs

Dividing your story into well-formed paragraphs gives you a great opportunity to try out different ways of organising the plot. I said at the start that paragraphs represent the panels, doors and windows of your narrative: just as an architect will design a beautiful and functional house by moving these elements around until they look and work best, so a writer can order and re-order paragraphs until they tell the best possible story.

Often the most important thing to consider, when deciding which paragraph should go where, is the logic of the plot. What information does the reader need first and which aspects should be held back to increase tension or build the action? In most cases it is best to tell your story in sequence. If you are experimenting with flashbacks, working with multiple perspectives or using a double time scheme, make sure that each one is internally consistent; each element of the plot progresses logically within its own development. It is one thing to intentionally mislead the reader – as is often the basis of crime or thriller fiction – but to inadvertently confuse is to risk them getting bored and giving up on your story.

Place related paragraphs together and check whether they progress logically. Try changing the order and see whether this enhances the effect you are looking for. If you have written several paragraphs of description followed by another set progressing the action, might it be better to intersperse them? Test whether your dialogue is correctly paragraphed by making sure you can tell who is speaking simply from the paragraphing of each character's speech, without tags.

It can take time to become really adept at using paragraphs to make your fiction sing, so practise forming strong and logical paragraphs, which link to each other and/or break up sections, with everything you write. Paragraphs are a vital tool for the writer and act as signposts for the reader. Learn to use them to build scenes and action, develop and reveal character, introduce your themes and settings and control the tension and progress of your plot.

# 15

# WRITING A SCENE

We've talked about the need to keep a balance between 'showing' and 'telling' in fiction writing, with an emphasis on showing the reader what is happening to your characters, linked by sections of telling. Most of the showing you do will be in **scenes**, while the telling is often described as **summary.**

I said before that creating scenes in fiction is similar to doing so in a screenplay. However, in my opinion a fiction writer has more work to do: while a scriptwriter creates the dialogue for actors to interpret, and offers stage directions for a designer and director to realise, a novelist or short story writer has to provide the whole experience themselves, in words which make the reader feel entirely immersed in the action and emotion.

## What defines a scene?

A scene portrays a point of tension within the story. It has to include at least one character and usually covers a single event that occurs during a defined length of time in a specific place. When you want to change time, place or point of view, a new scene is required.

Scenes take place in 'real time', whether they are told in the past, present or even future tense, and take the reader through the action sequentially. Most scenes contain a blend of action, dialogue and description, sometimes even some 'telling'.

Like your overall plot structure, each scene, even the very shortest, should have a beginning, a middle and an ending. Scenes can vary in size from a few sentences or exchanges of dialogue, to several pages or even a whole chapter. The reader's interest is best maintained by alternating scenes of different lengths, with very short ones – just like short paragraphs – used to shock or bring a sense of speed and urgency, and longer ones developing your characters, taking them through more complex action or interaction, and addressing your theme in more depth.

## What should a scene do?

A scene has to drive your plot forward. You may have written the most entertaining or poignant scene possible, but if it does not progress your story, it will have to go – or be re-written. Each scene should also have something to say about, or some relationship to, your theme. Even if the reader isn't consciously aware of this link, they will feel a lack of coherence if it's not there.

Similarly, every scene should reveal something or develop our understanding of one or more of the characters. If you find your characters themselves haven't progressed or the reader has learned nothing new about them by the end of a scene, it's back to the drawing board to introduce this element.

Most of all, a scene should be used to build tension. This means that, much like a plot line, each scene must start out with a character's goal; one or more characters want or need to achieve something, whether it's to get information from a witness, get to work on time or get their beloved into bed. The tension results from their failure to meet their aim, either temporarily – but then the achievement of one goal only leads to another, equally vital goal – or repeatedly.

The middle section of a scene embodies the conflict between the character's aim and whatever or whoever is preventing them from achieving it. That conflict doesn't have to be obvious – an argument, a fight, a physical impossibility – it can be a subtle personality clash, an inability to say aloud what he is thinking, not enough or the wrong information to get her to the right conclusion.

And the ending of a scene is always the cliff hanger of failure, which leads the reader on to the next scene or summary.

## Creating a scene

Just as you need to hook a reader at the opening of your story, so you do at the beginning of every scene. Start with some action – which can be dialogue – rather than 'telling' back story about how the characters got there. New fiction writers often feel a reader needs to know the details of how their characters arrive at the key points, such as what time they got up that day, what they decided to wear, what the weather was like and what kind of transport they used to get there.

Readers are quite capable of either filling in, or simply not needing, that sort of information. If, on re-reading a scene, you find you have written a long-winded introduction to the main action, be ruthless and cut it. Start at a high point of tension and, if necessary, weave in the other information later.

Whether you are narrating in the first or third person, a scene should remain consistent in its point of view. If you are writing as an omniscient narrator, you can potentially describe the reactions of everyone involved, but it can make for tauter prose and greater tension to stick with the view of one or two characters, leaving the reaction of others to another scene. When writing from multiple first person perspectives, stick with a single character's point of view in each individual scene.

Always keep in mind the screen analogy when writing a scene, and create for your reader as full an experience as if they were watching a movie. Your characters are constantly experiencing the setting, reacting to other characters, feeling emotions and thinking thoughts, as well as speaking and acting themselves. Your scenes will come alive if you describe all these aspects, remembering to write with and about all the senses – sight, hearing, touch, smell, taste, emotion and rational response.

## Alternating scenes

By definition, one scene cannot be followed by another that starts exactly where the first ended. The gap between scenes should always represent a passage of time, and this can sometimes usefully be covered by a 'summary', or passage of 'telling' before the next 'showing' scene.

To maintain your reader's interest, use scenes for contrast: long scenes should alternate with shorter scenes, action scenes with those of interior thought or dialogue, indoor scenes with outdoor scenes, and so on.

Manage scenes to keep your main plot and subplots moving forward at a good and even pace. Check that there is a varied pattern in the progression of your scenes, which might go something like: Main plot, Subplot 1, Main plot, Subplot 2, Main plot, Subplot 1, Subplot 2, Main plot, Subplot 2, Main Plot, Subplot 1... Your main plot should have a greater number of scenes than any of the subplots

The various plotlines may take place in different settings or from the point of view of different characters, so scheduling their appearances in regular, alternating scenes allows you to keep track of them and ensure they come together smoothly towards the end.

# 16

# MORE PUNCTUATION
# – SENSE AND SENSIBILITY

In my experience as an editor, too many fiction writers seem to think that the rules of grammar, and especially those of punctuation, just get in the way of their creativity. Nothing could be further from the case: punctuation is there to enable you to communicate your ideas clearly to your reader. Mispunctuation can not only make your writing hard to understand, it can completely change the sense of what you want to say.

This isn't an original example, but it makes the point:

A woman without her man is nothing

If you punctuate this sentence with a couple of commas to create a subclause in the middle, it means one thing:

A woman, *without her man*, is nothing.

However, if you use a colon for expansion and add a comma to separate an opening clause, without altering a single word it means almost exactly the opposite:

*A woman:* without her, *man is nothing.*

The best way to remember the right applications of the different punctuations marks – and there aren't that many of them, after all – is to limit the situations in which you should use them. If you've stuck a comma in a sentence but it doesn't seem to be for one of these three main uses, it probably shouldn't be there.

## Three Main Uses of Commas

### 1. Commas Contain Clauses

If in doubt about where to place commas in a sentence, remember the above title. Commas should *not* be used, as is often taught in school, simply to indicate where a pause occurs in spoken speech. Understanding where to place a comma correctly is more often about separating the subclause from the main clause of a sentence.

When the subclause (in italics below) is placed at the start or end of a sentence, it only needs one comma to separate it from the main clause:

*Despite having been neglected*, the garden was a riot of blossom.

The garden was a riot of blossom, *despite having been neglected*.

But when the subclause falls in the middle of a sentence, it needs a comma either side to enclose it:

The garden, *despite having been neglected*, was a riot of blossom.

In the sentence above, it would probably be better to use no commas at all than to put only one before, or one after, the subclause.

**2. Commas separate qualifying words and phrases** in a sentence in exactly the same way:

*However*, I'm delighted to say that... I'm delighted, *however*, to say that...

From my perspective, it looks like... It looks, from my perspective, like...

**3. Commas separate items in a simple list:**

When writing fiction it is important to be clear about your *plot, theme, characters, setting* and *writing style*.

As a general rule, don't put a comma before 'and'; always put a comma before 'but'.

Too many writers don't use semi-colons, that most delicate and subtle punctuation mark, because they don't know what they are for or where to place them. (Equally, too many writers use them, wrongly believing they know where to use them, and cause a lot of work for editors.) As there are only two main uses, it's not too hard to remember.

## Link and Separate – the Only Two Uses for the Semi-colon

**1. Semi-colons link two related clauses** which could otherwise be joined by a conjunction or separated by a period/full stop.

So, you might write:

I love Paris. It is a beautiful city.

Or:

I love Paris because it is a beautiful city.

But more subtle and interesting is:

I love Paris; it is a beautiful city.

*Don't* use a semi-colon to link two *unrelated* clauses – 'I love Paris; let's have pizza tonight.' would not be correct. *Don't* use a semi-colon *and* a conjunction to link two clauses – 'I love Paris; because it's a beautiful city.' is also incorrect.

**2. Semi-colons separate items on a complex list** (a list with long items and items that have internal punctuation, such as a comma).

> Breakfast consisted of *newly laid, hard-boiled eggs; grilled, smoked bacon; mushrooms fried in butter; and wholegrain, toasted slices of bread.*

In complex lists like this I would put a semi-colon before the final 'and', unlike at the end of a simple list separated by commas.

Most people are pretty secure in their use of colons, though I have seen them used in place of a semi-colon, so let me remind you of...

## The Three Main Uses for Colons

**1. Definition or expansion** of an initial statement

> I felt a sudden twinge: the wound in my knee was playing up.

In this case, the phrase following the colon should start with a lower case word, unless it's 'I' or a proper name; or if the definition/expansion continues for more than one sentence.

## 2. To set up a quotation

Polonius tells Laertes: '… to thine own self be true.'

If the quote is more than a sentence long, it should start on a new line following the colon, and form an indented paragraph not enclosed in quotation marks.

## 3. To introduce a list

This recipe requires the following ingredients: 3 eggs, 6 oz flour, 6 oz sugar and 6 oz butter.

Items can also be numbered or bulleted following a colon. If the introductory phrase does not stand alone as a sentence, a colon is not required. *This recipe requires 3 eggs, 6 oz flour…*

If you really want to irritate a reader or an editor, putting your apostrophes in the wrong place is a quick and easy way to do it. The first of these is obvious, but *do not* mess up your 'its' and your 'it's'. And take serious note of how to use a possessive apostrophe to mean what you intend it to.

'To those who care about punctuation, a sentence such as "Thank God its Friday" (without the apostrophe) rouses feelings not only of despair but of violence. The confusion of the possessive "its" (no apostrophe) with the contractive "it's" (with apostrophe) is an unequivocal signal of illiteracy and sets off a Pavlovian "kill" response in the average stickler.'

LYNNE TRUSS, 'EATS, SHOOTS & LEAVES:
THE ZERO TOLERANCE APPROACH TO PUNCTUATION'

## The Two Main Uses of the Apostrophe

**1. To show where a word has been contracted** and a letter(s) left out

*Don't* for 'do not'; *she'll* for 'she will'; *he's* for 'he is' or 'he has'.

Simple enough, apart from using an apostrophe with the word 'it'. The possessive, *its,* has no apostrophe; only put an apostrophe in *it's* when it's a contraction of 'it is'.

**2. To denote possession – apostrophe+s**

*Anna's book* (the book owned by Anna); *In a week's time* (within the period of a week).

If the word ends in 's', whether it is plural (books) or is singular but ends in 's' (James), add the **apostrophe alone:** *The books' covers* (covers of the books); *James'* *coat* (the coat belonging to James). Plurals that do not end in 's' (eg, women, children), take apostrophe+s in the possessive: *the women's bags, the children's toys.*

**Don't** use an apostrophe to make a plural, even of acronyms or dates. The plural of PC is *PCs*, not PC's; the flower power decade is *the 1960s*, not the 1960's. The Smith family are *the Smiths*, not *the Smith's*.

Finally, let's look at those alternative sentence endings, question and exclamation marks. It may seem obvious, but again it's surprising how often question marks are misplaced and added at the end of statements that are not questions. As for exclamation marks – delete, delete, delete. A full length book rarely needs more than half a dozen exclamation marks in the whole manuscript; many more tells an editor or publisher that this is an amateur writer. As with adjectives and adverbs, less is much, much more. Your choice of words and writing style should make it clear to a reader where your emphases fall.

**Question marks** should only be used after direct questions:

How many copies will my book sell?

'I wonder how many copies my book will sell.' is a statement, not a question and should not have a question mark.

When it comes to exclamation marks, F. Scott Fitzgerald says it all:

> 'Cut out all those exclamation points.
> An exclamation point is like
> laughing at your own joke.'

If you really think one is necessary, make it one – never two or more. And if you must use both a question mark and exclamation mark together, it should be that way round: ?!

# 17

# DEALING WITH WRITERS' BLOCK

Inevitably I have found this section a hard one to get written.

Why do we sometimes find it impossible to start, or continue, our story; to see the way forward from a particular point in our plot; to identify the right actions and dialogue to develop a character; to get our thoughts to flow and find the right words to express them?

Of course there are myriad reasons, probably as many as there are writers, but some common situations exist in which many of us experience writers' block. I am hoping that, if you have come thus far with me, you are not stuck at the primary level of writers' block: the 'I want to write a story, but I can't come up with the right idea' stage. Even if you are, taking the structured approach of doggedly working through the initial steps of outlining your story, developing your characters, defining your theme and clarifying your setting, should get you moving.

> ### 'The art of writing is the art of applying the seat of the pants to the seat of the chair.'
>
> #### MARY HEATON VORSE

When you do feel stuck at the start of a project, your most critical task is to establish a **writing schedule**. Form the habit of writing at the same time every day (or as regularly as possible), in the same place and with the same routine and props – for instance a specific mug of coffee. The more frequently repeated elements you can get your brain to associate with the act of writing, the more habituated it will become to working creatively on cue.

> ### 'Authors with a mortgage never get writers' block.'
>
> #### MAVIS CHEEK

Along with establishing the habit of regular writing, cultivating the attitude of writing as a **job of work**, with projects, targets, reviews and deadlines, also mitigates against the mindset that allows you to get stuck in your story. Most working people do not have the luxury of being unproductive: journalists, speechwriters, business writers and other professional scribes would lose their livelihood if they allowed themselves to succumb to writers' block. Even if you aren't being paid for your writing at this stage, and don't have an external deadline, think and behave as if you are and have.

> **'Imagination is like a muscle. I found out that the more I wrote the bigger it got.'**
> PHILIP JOSÉ FARMER

When you first start writing, stamina may be an issue, and if you can't focus for long periods, your story may falter too. The only answer to this is to treat writing as you might an **exercise programme**: schedule regular short sessions at first, write what comes easily, and slowly build up the quantity and quality of your output. Congratulate yourself on your achievements and don't knock yourself for not achieving your targets. Just keep going and don't give up.

> **'If you get stuck, get away from your desk. Take a walk, take a bath, go to sleep, make a pie, draw, listen to music, meditate, exercise; whatever you do, don't just stick there scowling at the problem.'**
> HILARY MANTEL

I won't presume to improve on the words of multi-award-winning Ms Mantel, but I will explain that intermittent writers' block can occur when your conscious brain gets overloaded with material – information, options, thoughts, emotions – and won't function creatively until you let it process and file some of this data. Just as sleeping allows the day's experiences to be processed into the subconscious, and you often awake with a solution to a problem that seemed intractable the day before, so a change of activity, especially from mental to physical, gives time and space for story processing.

Some authors swear by the efficacy of a session of vigorous exercise to divert them for sufficient time, and get their re-oxygenated brains firing again. Even stepping away from your screen for long enough to put a load in the washing machine can break the grip of writers' block, and provide a 'reboot' to the creative function. Walking (especially in natural surroundings) and meditation, though, seem especially beneficial to many writers. Both activities, though gently physical, allow the mind to enter a creative state where thoughts and emotions can surface in a free-flowing and seemingly automatic way.

### 'If I don't write to empty my mind, I go mad.'
**LORD BYRON**

This is because the conscious mind is limited by what it can hold in short-term memory and the slow progression of rational thought. The subconscious, by contrast, holds a lifetime of experiences and emotions, and makes connections in a far more nimble and esoteric fashion. Writers have to learn to use both mental states: accessing the subconscious for inspiration and working the conscious for the 'perspiration' of story-making. Developing a facility to flip between these states is the long-term cure to writers' block. Being able to combine these states can lead to 'flow' – the ultimate creative state.

But in the short term, and when writers' block strikes out of the blue, take tips from and be inspired by others who have overcome it. They all, essentially, say the same thing:

Get started.

> ### 'A lot of people talk about writing. The secret is to write, not talk.'
> JACKIE COLLINS

> ### 'Prescription for writer's block: begin.'
> CYNTHIA OZICK

'You don't need to wait for inspiration to write. It's easier to be inspired while writing than while not writing…'

JOSIP NOVAKOVICH

Write. Write anything.

'The beautiful part of writing is you don't have to get it right first time, unlike, say, a brain surgeon.'

ROBERT CORMIER

'Don't talk about it. Don't get a lovely studio or a beautiful desk. Just do it.'

NATALIE GOLDBERG

Keep writing.

'Writers write while dreamers procrastinate.'

BEZA KOSOVA

'A professional writer is an amateur who didn't quit.'

RICHARD BACH

# PART THREE

# REVIEWING & EDITING

# 18

# REVIEWING ACT ONE – THE BEGINNING

Since we finished working through the structure of your story, we have looked at your narrative voice, getting your reader hooked early on, 'showing' as opposed to 'telling', writing dialogue for your characters, and the nitty-gritty of sentence and paragraph construction. During this time you may have started to write your story and put some of this into practice.

Whether you are writing a full length novel, a novella or short story – even flash fiction – all storytelling is built on a three act structure: beginning, middle and end.

So if you've been writing the beginning of your story, which I defined earlier as two sections: the **Trigger** (or inciting incident which initiates the action of the plot); and the **Quest Begins** (in which the hero/ine or main characters set off on their physical or emotional journey) what should you have included?

Here's a checklist:

☐ You have started story with, or included very early on, a dramatic incident which grabbed the readers' attention. This might be a time to go back and check whether you can edit out some of your opening paragraphs or pages and embed background information into later action.

☐ You have introduced the protagonist(s) and most of the central characters.

☐ You have set up the status quo of their opening position(s), from where the plot will soon move them out of their comfort zone.

☐ You have given the reader reasons to like, or at least engage with, the main characters.

☐ You have initiated the major plot line, the central 'problem' or 'issue', the solving or resolving of which the story revolves around, and established how high the stakes are for the protagonist(s) of achieving their quest.

☐ You have got the ball rolling on one or more subplots – either directly or by foreshadowing them.

☐ You have established the setting of your story – including the era, country, society and ethos.

☐ You have introduced the 'villain' or nemesis of the hero(ine).

☐ You have embedded your theme within the opening chapters of the story.

This could be a good time to let one or a couple of trusted readers (sometimes called beta readers), and/or a writing mentor, look at your work. Be clear about what sort of feedback you want from them: it must be honest, specific and constructive, including positive reactions as well as improvements they think you could make.

Ask them to tell you:

- Their overall reaction – and especially whether they wanted to read on to find out what was going to happen next.

- How they felt about the main character(s). Did they love, hate, engage with or feel irritated by them? Specifically why?

- What they thought the story was going to consist of (you want them to be half right, but not to guess the entire plot at the stage).

- Whether they had a clear picture of the world you have established for your story.

- If they found it easy to read – in the sense of not being distracted by poor grammar, spelling, punctuation, or hard-to-follow action (bearing in mind that this is only your first draft).

- If there were any obvious plot holes or inconsistencies.

- What they enjoyed most.

- What they would most like you to change.

In summary, Act One is a preparation for the reader. In it, the world of the story should be established and the protagonist should meet most of the other characters, especially their enemy/ies. It is where the reader must understand what the main problem or issue of the story is going to be, engage emotionally with the hero/ine(s) and become aware, even subliminally, of the theme of your book.

The most important aspect of the **Beginning** two sections is to draw the reader in and ensure they want to know how the story is going to turn out.

# 19

# REVIEWING ACT TWO – THE MIDDLE

## Part One

If you have been speeding your way through Act Two and are approaching, or have reached, the halfway mark – which is also the halfway point of your story – we should take a look at how it's going.

The central section of your story is also the longest; Act Two should be at least twice as long as each of Act One and Act Three and contain most of the action. For that reason, and because it works best in terms of classic story-telling structure, it's helpful to break Act Two into two parts.

In Act One, you set up the protagonist(s) and the problem they had to solve. You did this in two sections we called **The Trigger** – the event that motivated your main character's journey; and **Quest Begins** – in which your hero(es) take the crucial, even if reluctant, step to seek the answer or resolve the problem that has been set them.

The first half of Act Two moves on to **Quest Continues** and **Reversal 1**. These two sections combined can be the most exciting and compelling part of the narrative; the best way to make them so is to check whether you have included your own version of some of these tried and tested elements.

## A New World

The beginning of the second act of a book is often where the protagonist(s) enter a new world, whether that is a physical place or setting, interaction with a new group of people, taking on a different role, or operating with a changed emotional outlook.

This might be prompted by setting out on a physical journey, as in classical legends; entering the world of the villain in crime or spy fiction; starting a new job, project or career; becoming part of a beloved's or antagonist's social environment; going on holiday; or quite literally finding themselves in a magical place, as in *Alice In Wonderland*, *The Lion, The Witch And The Wardrobe*, or *Harry Potter*.

*What kind of new world has your hero entered at the start of Act Two?*

## The Gatekeeper

Introducing a character who serves the archetypal function of a 'threshold guardian' or 'guardian at the gate' of this new world offers useful opportunities. It could be a boss who promotes the hero or gives them the project; a mentor who offers advice or a warning – the latter being a well-used, but often effective, technique for generating suspense; or a character, perhaps a confidant, who has already entered the new world and invites them in or gives them access.

Alternatively, the Gatekeeper may try to prevent the protagonist entering the new world, either for their own good, because they may know something the hero doesn't, or because they want to prevent the quest taking place. The Gatekeeper may be on the hero's side or on the villain's, or, most intriguingly, they may be one masquerading as the other.

*Have you made use of a Gatekeeper to move your main characters into their new world, with advice or a warning?*

## The Plan

Early in the second act, the hero must formulate their plan. The reader discovered their goal in Act One, but now they need to know how the protagonist intends to go about solving the problem or answering the question. Of course the initial plan will be more straightforward than the quest turns out to require, so the hero will have to change and escalate it throughout the story, but Act Two, Part One is where the first version of the plan is revealed.

*Have you made the reader aware of the protagonist's plan of action in this section of your story?*

## Complication

Although the initial quest is given to the main character(s) in Act One, early on in Act Two they must learn something which complicates the question or problems they are out to solve. Although the hero(es) should only now discover it, the complication will work best if it is a piece of the back-story that has remained hidden until now. The protagonist must then start to try solving this bigger, more complicated problem, which is not one of the reversals they experience, but may be something they learn from the Gatekeeper, or arises during their Initiation.

*Have you thrown a red hot spanner into the works in the first half of Act Two, to complicate the Plan?*

## Initiation or Training

When the protagonist enters the new world, s/he will have to learn new skills and gain fresh knowledge to put the plan into practice and deal with the places, people and problems that face them. Their initiation into the new world, or training they need to undergo, often performs a useful function in moving the action forward, introducing information and characters, as well as giving the reader knowledge about a real or fictitious setting or period, with particular reference to your theme.

*What is your protagonist having to learn, or be initiated into, in order to get going on their quest?*

## Building the Team

The initiation period also gives a writer the opportunity to gather the team that will support the hero(es) in achieving their quest. The training allows you opportunities to demonstrate the strengths and weaknesses of these characters, which will be tested through the later reversals, and their relationships to the protagonist and each other.

*Who have you put in place to support your protagonist through their quest and what are their interesting quirks and characteristics?*

## Moving Target

In direct conflict to, or competition with, the hero's plan, the reader also needs to become aware of the antagonist's goals in the first half of Act Two. You may have actually shown the forces of evil plotting their moves, or you may wish to reveal only elements or the effect of the antagonists' plan.

Both techniques are effective, but what is crucial is that the reader sees the villain start to act in opposition to the hero. Whether or not the heroes realise who is attacking them, their enemy must be shown as present and active; a constantly moving target requiring the hero's response; a ticking time bomb.

*How is your villain making their presence felt in the first half of Act Two?*

## Genre definition

The first part of Act Two is where you have the greatest opportunity to use the distinctive story-telling tools of your chosen genre. In a crime story your protagonist can question witnesses, suggest and eliminate suspects, collate and follow clues, voice their theory. This is where you can also set up red herrings and false trails. If you are writing a romance, the hero can have an initial encounter with her object of desire, learn about their negative past, come up against her rival. If you are writing science fiction or fantasy, now is the time to develop the physical, technical, social and moral aspects of your setting.

*Have you made it clear to the reader (and potential publisher or agent) that you know how your genre of story works, even if you want to subvert the norms later?*

## The Midpoint

When you reach the middle of Act Two, your protagonist must experience her or his first major reversal: a midpoint climax which is often a set-piece action scene or major emotional unraveling. It might be a sex scene or a comedy scene, or both in a romantic comedy. It could be an unexpected crime, a revelation about a team member, or an earth-shattering event or experience. Whatever this reversal is, make sure that it has acted as a major game-changer for your hero(es).

The end of Act Two, Part One is when the protagonist has a revelation, suddenly seeing what it is about themselves that has to change in order to achieve their goal, and leading to a new learning curve through the second part of Act Two, where they struggle with their past attitudes, behaviour, morals, understanding or expectations. It is a point of no return, which can come out of a huge defeat, a loss, or an action by the villain which means that 'now it's personal'.

*What happens to your protagonist at the end of Act Two, Part One that changes their thinking as they move into Part Two?*

## Part Two

In the first half of your story, the main characters have identified and set out on their quest, entered a new world, gained supporters, appreciated who their antagonists are and arrived at their first serious reversal. Up until this midpoint they have mainly been dealing with external forces in the battle to achieve the goal they have set themselves.

We said that the first half of Act Two should end with a midpoint crisis that functions as a game-changer for your hero(es). So now your protagonist(s) head into the second half of your story with even more determination and a new direction.

The following elements should characterise Act Two, Part Two:

## Emotional insight

The first major reversal that occurred in the middle of your story should affect your hero(es) emotionally, and change their feelings and thinking, as well as their behaviour, for the second half. It should have triggered a revelation, to some extent about themselves, though it may have also given them insight about someone else, such as their beloved or their antagonist.

## Quest revised

This crisis should also change the nature of the quest, upping the stakes and/or adding to its difficulty.

The midpoint crisis could be a low moment, when all seems lost; or it can offer the first glimmer of hope that your protagonist(s) will achieve their goal. In either case, the question for reader and heroes at the beginning of the second half of Act Two is, 'What now?' This is where you begin to put pressure on your main character(s), not just in terms of their new insights and personal development, but in the increased difficulty of achieving their goal, which has shifted or become more complex. Their plan will need to be revised in the light of their new awareness.

## Gather in subplots

Up to the halfway mark, your main plot and subplots may have been running independently, with only a few clues thrown to the reader about how they interconnect. In the third quarter of the story it is time to start weaving them closer, otherwise you will end up with too many loose ends to bring together in Act Three.

This is a good time to go back to the beginning and list all the stories you have started, characters you have introduced and clues you have dropped that will need to be brought to a satisfying conclusion in a seamless, coherent and sometimes unexpected way.

## Focus on the main plot

Despite the greater complexity of this section and the need to draw in your subplots, don't lose your focus on the main plot. Keep checking in with your story 'bible' to follow through on the hero's quest that you set up in Act One. Achieving this quest is the promise you made to your reader at the beginning, and if it starts to lose clarity, they will lost interest and their trust in you, their story-teller.

## Keep building tension

The tension through Act Two, part two, must build with the complexity of the story. Keep in mind the two-step structure you have still to play out: build to a second reversal, and keep building, in pace and tension, to the third and final reversal – at which point it must appear that the protagonist(s) simply cannot achieve their goal.

This means there must be a clear line connecting the twists of the main plot and subplot(s), and that the stakes are raised at every turn. You should be increasing physical and psychological stress for the hero(es) and the reader, through short action sequences, snappy dialogue and engaging description.

Mix it up, use your techniques, keep the surprises coming.

## Look out – he's behind you!

The third quarter of your story is where the antagonist really comes into her or his own; s/he seems to be one step ahead of the hero(es), getting the girl or guy, his or her revenge, winning the battle, escaping the trap. Be careful, though, that the baddies don't steal the limelight. Often the villains are more fun to write than the good guys, but keep in mind that your story always belongs to the hero(es). Hold the balance with good and evil neck and neck to the final reversal.

## The Black Moment

At the very end of Act Two, despite all the action and interaction, the protagonists' journey takes a downward turn, ending in the end-of-act reversal – the hero's Black Moment. Suddenly all seems lost: the quest is ruined; the goal is unachievable.

Either something deeply shocking has happened – the hero loses a main supporter, the antagonist's trick succeeds, the protagonists themselves fail; or the fiasco that has always looked likely to the reader comes to pass. Another way of playing this is to give your reader more information than your hero: you reveal the truth to them, but the protagonist's ignorance means they might just give up on their goal.

Whichever way you have played your story, this moment requires all the drama you can give it – the main characters are in danger or despair; the villains are triumphant.

The Black Moment is the essential precursor to the Climax of Act Three where all starts to become clear and you can bring everything together.

**20**

# REVIEWING ACT THREE – THE END

### 'Act 3 begins with the unexpected and ends with the long-anticipated.'
#### RIDLEY PEARSON

The two sections that make up Act 3 of your story, as we identified them in the initial plot structure, are **Climax** and **Resolution**. The Climax should be full of unexpected events; and the Resolution should have been, even if subconsciously, long-anticipated by the reader.

To conclude your tale in a way that is still keeping the reader on the edge of their seat after the roller coaster action of Act Two, you need to maintain the element of surprise; at the same time, to fulfil your contract with the reader, you have to keep the 'promise' you made to them in Act One. In general, this will mean that your hero(es) succeed in their quest, even if it is not exactly the one they set out with initially.

## Achieving the Climax

To achieve the third act Climax, your protagonist(s) must make a final, right decision and be acting out of the new knowledge and personal values that they have developed since the midpoint reversal of Act Two. It is called the Climax because this must be the scene, or series of scenes, in which the tensions of the main plot reach their most intense point, and the key questions are finally answered. It may be that you allow the reader to recognise what these answers are before the main characters catch on.

The Climax should be, literally or metaphorically, the final confrontation between the hero and the villain. Often it comes down to just these two characters: the generals of opposing armies; the lover and her/his rival; the sleuth and the criminal; the superhero and the nemesis. In some stories this might be because in the final reversal of Act Two, the protagonist(s) lose their mentor, companion or team members. In this final clash, one or more of the main characters' lives should in some sense hang in the balance.

## Moving to Resolution

The Climax will also feature your subplots, as they feed into the final outcomes, though you can leave some loose ends to be tied down in the Resolution. This very last section gives the readers the satisfying experience of following your trail to its denouement; the ending they have anticipated from the start, but without knowing how it was going to come about.

Some stories, of course, have tragic endings, where the hero might learn a lesson, gain knowledge or develop understanding, yet, at the last, fails the quest, or even dies. Nonetheless, the way you bring this about should also keep your initial promise with the reader, even if in a less obvious way.

## Trouble-shooting

One problem you might find with your third act is that if you have created strong dynamic characters who have grown and developed during the story, they may have taken the plot into territory beyond your original plans. In this case, you will need to ensure it still ties back into a satisfactory resolution. If you can't force your characters to behave as you first envisaged, you will have to carefully rework parts of Act Three.

Another challenge that Act Three can present is that your story either peters out with a whimper, or you find you can't pull all the strands together in a satisfactory way. The reasons for either of these can be that you haven't fully answered the dramatic problems, or questions, that you set up in Act One. This is what I mean by not fulfilling your contract with the reader, and what will leave them feeling unsatisfied.

> ## 'If you have a problem with the third act, the real problem is in the first act.'
> **BILLY WILDER**

To make sure you have got the ending to your story right, go back and look at Act One to check what expectations you have set up for your reader; then review what happens in Act Three and ensure you have fulfilled and reflected back each one.

### Act One/Act Three Checklist:

☐ *Act One*: you opened with dramatic incident which grabbed the readers' attention.

☐ *Act Three*: a similarly dramatic event explains, balances and closes the earlier one.

☐ *Act One:* You introduced the protagonist(s) and most of the central characters.

☐ *Act Three:* You resolve the issues of all the central characters and close all their individual stories.

☐ *Act One:* The protagonists are in a comfort zone which they leave quickly and spend Act Two in increasing discomfort.

☐ *Act Three:* The hero(es) have moved into a new, and better, comfort zone, whether physical, emotional or intellectual.

☐ *Act One:* The main characters displayed engaging, and probably likeable, characteristics – soon to be challenged by events.

☐ *Act Three:* If they have grown and developed through Act Two, now is the point where they regroup and display their new, positive attributes to the reader.

☐ *Act One:* The central problem or issue to be resolved (the Quest) was established.

☐ *Act Three:* The Quest is achieved; the problem is definitely resolved; all questions are answered.

☐ *Act One:* Your subplots were initiated – either directly or by foreshadowing.

☐ *Act Three:* The subplots are woven back into the central plotline; all loose ends are tied in, in a way that balances their introduction.

☐ *Act One:* You established the setting of your story – including the era, country, society and ethos.

☐ *Act Three:* If the setting has changed or developed, you have established the new environment in as much detail as the original.

☐ *Act One:* You introduced the 'villain' or nemesis of the protagonist.

☐ *Act Three:* The antagonist's plot arc is complete; the reader feels satisfied that s/he has received his or her just deserts.

☐ *Act One:* You embedded your theme within the opening chapters of the story.

☐ *Act Three:* You are confident your theme has been carried through the action of Act Two and, in Act Three, your ending makes a strong point about that theme.

I suggested that you ask one or more trusted readers look at Act One before you continued writing, and gave you feedback. As you review Act Three, check that the comments and suggestions with which you agreed have been incorporated. Now your story is complete, it is time to go back to your beta readers and ask them to review it through to the end – although you may choose to leave this until after you have edited your manuscript, which is what we will be looking at next.

# 21

# EDITING

'Editing is like pruning the rose bush you
thought was so perfect and beautiful
until it overgrew the garden.'

LARRY ENRIGHT

## Take a break

Finishing the first draft of your story is a huge
achievement; you should congratulate yourself, then
take a break. Start planning, even writing, your next
fiction project or turn your attention to something
other than writing for a few weeks. You should do
this, not because the story you've been working on is
finished, but because you need to put chronological
and emotional distance between you and it before
you can come back and edit it with an objective eye.

## Get feedback

Even though what you have completed so far may be only the first of several drafts (yes, I'm afraid the editing phase can be just as time-consuming and difficult as the initial writing), it is well worth asking trusted beta readers, or a professional editor, to read and give you feedback before you start the next phase. Perhaps the most useful pointers they can give you are to note where in the story they begin to lose interest, disengage with your character(s), feel confused or that the plot lacks credibility. Accept any negative responses from honest readers at this stage as a gift; they may save you from rejection by agents or publishers, or bad reviews from critics or paying readers.

## Self critique

When, after at least three weeks break, you come back to edit your first draft, print out a hard copy for extra separation. Try to read it at times and in the way you would read fiction for pleasure, but do so with a pen in hand and, like your beta readers, note your emotional responses especially. Write yourself a critique, as if for a writer friend, particularly about the bigger issues you have become aware of, such as structural problems, character flaws, subplots that don't work, loose ends that still need tying in – anything that feels unsatisfactory or takes you, as a reader rather than writer, out of your fictional world.

Only at this point will you have an idea of the size and complexity of your editing task. You should expect it to be as long or big a project as the initial writing. Whether your plot hangs together, but your style and grammar need a nitpicking edit; or you realise that a considerable structural overhaul is required, don't be daunted. This is the heavy-lifting of fiction writing, and the work that will build your muscle and technique as a story-teller.

## Be systematic

While everyone should work in the way that best suits their methods and thought processes, it is crucial to be systematic as well as creative when editing. Try to stop thinking like the writer you are and take on the mindset of a professional editor. This means stepping back from your investment in all aspects of your story and looking for what might be missing – a crucial scene, a key piece of information in the right place… Focus on cutting out distractions from the main story – pointless dialogue, unnecessary characters, sub-plots that don't tie into the theme… Be systematic – and ruthless.

> 'Put down everything that comes into your head and then you're a writer. But an author is one who can judge his own stuff's worth, without pity, and destroy most of it.'
>
> COLETTE

## First the big picture

It makes sense to start with the big picture aspects before drilling down to sentence- and word-level fine details. This is because revisions in any area, but especially in story-wide issues, will very likely lead to change throughout the manuscript. It's clear enough that if you find a problem in Act One, you will need to work it through the action of Act Two and into the resolution. If, though, you pick up on a glitch in Act Three, you may have to work backwards to the moment you introduced this character or set up that thread. And if your midpoint reversal turns out to be flawed, it will need reworking both before and after.

Big picture areas include those we worked on to create your story 'bible'. Check that your plot and structure are really working and re-read the sections taking you through the three act structure. Character, theme and setting are all big picture elements that need to be questioned thoroughly by your editing self. If your beta readers' comments resonate with your own intuition, don't be afraid to make changes, major or minor.

## Then the detail

Once you have finessed your story in terms of these wider issues, it's time to edit the manuscript for fine detail. If you have made some major revisions and done some extensive rewriting, it could be helpful to take another break before you start the close work on syntax and style.

In addition to checking against the information in the sections on scene writing, paragraph and sentence construction, as well as grammar and punctuation, make sure you:

- Check your facts – dates, science, events, real places or people…

- Vary your vocabulary – try not to use the same word more than once in a paragraph, let alone a sentence; find different ways to express yourself.

- Make each sentence and every word count – shorten, delete and rephrase for accuracy and simplicity (more on this shortly).

- Read aloud for rhythm – if any sentence doesn't feel quite right, read it aloud to discover where it's losing pace or tying itself in knots.

- Get up to speed with grammar – if you're not already a grammar nerd, buy one, or more, handbooks on grammar and punctuation and look up anything you're not sure of. Learn the rules and remember to apply them: it's slow going at first, but it will improve your writing – and editing – immeasurably. Clarity of expression leads to clarity of thought.

**'Edit your manuscript until your fingers bleed and you have memorized every last word. Then, when you are certain you are on the verge of insanity... edit one more time!'**

**C.K. WEBB**

When you reach the end of the self-editing process, re-read, ask others to read and feedback. Repeat the process if necessary. As many times as required. And when you have come to the end of your own editing abilities, consider seriously paying or begging a professional editor to review and polish your manuscript. As any successful author knows, if you are going to publish your story, or try to get it traditionally published, this is an investment you should not skimp on.

# 22

# TIGHTER WRITING

If there's one thing that divides the amateur from the professional fiction writer, it's the tautness of their prose style. Amateur writers' sentences often meander, twist and turn; they use many more words than required; and over-complicate their syntax in an effort to sound sophisticated. This can end up confusing readers, as well as slowing down the action of their story. An agent or commissioning editor will reject a manuscript with writing like this before they reach the bottom of the first page.

> 'To write well, express yourself like the common people, but think like a wise man.'
>
> ARISTOTLE

Seasoned writers, on the other hand, create crisp, elegant sentences in which every single word is precise and necessary, which have correct grammar and functional punctuation. They will make sure, through several drafts, rewrites and self-edits, that each phrase delivers its message with the fewest and the simplest, though most apposite, words. This makes their writing easy to read and dense with meaning – a fully satisfying experience.

## What is Loose Writing?

While tight writing is so well-honed that you could not remove or change a single word without altering the meaning or spoiling the rhythm, loose writing is full of extra and unnecessary articles, repetition, passive verbs, woolly words and wordy phrases. If you try to read loose writing aloud, it will be hard to make sense of sentences, to find a good rhythm and emphasise the right words.

This is not something you need to worry about in your first draft. If getting your story out fast and furiously is the best way for you, do it. You can come back and tighten up the style in a second, third and fourth draft. Getting every paragraph, sentence and phrase concise and precise is hard work, and may take longer than writing the story in the first place.

## Five Tighter Writing Tips

Here are five questions to check against every sentence as you revise:

## 1. Have you used the simplest word?

It's easy when we write to try and be too clever; to imagine that a short, everyday word isn't good enough for the readers of our fiction. We can make the mistake of picking fancy, longer words which are less accurate and distract from the flow. Choose the shortest, simplest word which will do the job, and reserve the longer, more abstruse ones for when you really need them.

Use *so* rather than *accordingly; begin* or *start* are better than *commence; size* is at least as good as *magnitude*; and please, never use words like *sub-optimal* instead of *worse* – unless you have a character whose dialogue tic is to speak in management jargon.

## 2. Is every word necessary?

We are lax about language when we talk and our instinct is often to write as we speak, packing in our usual superfluous verbiage, even if not the ums, ers and 'you know what I means'. Examine each sentence and eliminate every unnecessary word; combine sentences to remove repetition and to make the writing dense; divide a long, rambling sentence into two or three more compact ones.

Imagine trimming the fat off your sentences with a nice, sharp butcher's knife until you've got a lean piece of steak, by cutting some typically overused phrases down to a single word, like these:

Are in possession of (have); at this point in time (now); is able to (can); in spite of the fact that (although); in the not too distant future (soon); on a weekly basis (weekly); in the vicinity of (near).

### 3. Are your verbs active and direct?

The active voice is almost always simpler and shorter than the passive; it also tends to be a less pretentious way of constructing a sentence.

*The door was opened and the guests were greeted by the butler* is longer and more pompous than *The butler opened the door and greeted the guests.*

Be wary of sentences containing 'There are/were/is/was…' and '…who were/are/was/is'. These introductory and descriptive phrases are usually redundant. Rather than *There were some groups of teenagers who were chattering to each other as they walked down the street*, write *Groups of chattering teenagers walked down the street.*

## 4. Can you cut out adverbs, adjectives and qualifiers?

### 'The road to hell is paved with adverbs.'
STEPHEN KING

Adverbs rarely add value to a sentence. If you need to add impact to a weak verb, choose a stronger verb and ditch the adverb. Rather than, *Her fingers moved lightly over the typewriter keys*, write *Her fingers skimmed the typewriter keys*. This is also a way of ensuring you choose the most accurate wording.

Adverbs are at their worst in dialogue tags: *'I won't do it!' Emma shouted angrily* is weakened because both her words and the fact that Emma shouted already suggest anger. *'I won't do it!' Emma shouted* is both more powerful and pithier.

Mark Twain said it all – and with commendable brevity – about adjectives:

### 'As to the adjective, when in doubt, strike it out.'
MARK TWAIN

He also made a similar point about qualifiers – very, rather, quite, some, etc:

> **'Substitute 'damn' every time you're inclined to write 'very': your editor will delete it and the writing will be just as it should be.'**
>
> **MARK TWAIN**

## 5. Have you been specific?

Tight, and engaging writing never uses the words like 'get', 'something' or 'thing'.

*Something made Tom get some things and put them in his bag* makes a poor fiction sentence. Readers will want to know what Tom took with him – clothes, documents, plumbing equipment? – and why he was motivated to do so. Depending on which of these it might be, 'got' needs to be replaced by 'took from the wardrobe', picked off his desk' or 'scrabbled in the cupboard under the sink for…'. Even the 'bag' is too general: a rucksack, briefcase or toolbox is what readers need to visualise this scene.

> *Catching sight of Emma's post-it note on the fridge made Tom scrabble in the cupboard under the sink for his plumbing tools and shove them into his toolbox.*

Although this is longer, it is always the specifics of what, when, how, where and why that move the action on, reveal more about the theme and build characters. If you catch yourself using general words, it will because your thinking and imagination has become vague. Go back into a scene and, using all your senses, check each word and rewrite every sentence so they paint a clear, specific and accurate picture for the reader.

# 23

# FICTION WRITING NO NOS

While you're reviewing the four major sections of your story, carrying out a close edit, or indeed while you're writing, keep an eye out for these fiction no nos that will make your work appear amateurish and turn off readers, agents, publishers and editors alike. Try your hardest to weed out these easy to make, but basic blunders:

## Too Much Information

In shorter stories, especially, you can overload the writing and the reader with too much information, which is distracting and slows down your plot. Where you come across patches of very detailed description or dialogue, interrogate it word by word, sentence by sentence, asking whether this information actually furthers the plot, draws out the theme, develops character or gives a sense of time and place.

A couple of well chosen sentences can set a scene in the reader's imagination. A minor character doesn't need to have their appearance and attitudes outlined if they don't have a significant role in the story. Quality of information is much more telling than quantity and you can rely on readers' imaginations to add light and shade around your precise and colourful brushstrokes.

## Data Dumping

Different to excess information, this one can trip you up especially at the beginning of the story or when introducing a new character or situation. This is where you feel the reader needs to know a whole lot of back story, or the minutiae of someone's character and, just to make sure they get your point, you'll tell them up front.

Worst of all is the 'As you know…' dump, where you give the reader information on the pretext of one character telling another a whole load of facts they are clearly already aware of. Is it likely that you'd say to your closest friend, 'As you know, Emma, I married my husband Dave six years ago and we used to be very happy, but since the birth of our twins, Tim and Tom, things haven't been so easy…'? Never tell characters what they already know.

Think about real life: when you meet someone, or go somewhere, for the first time, you don't get presented with a CV, or a behaviour guide. You pick up information gradually, through all your senses and intuition, which allows you to piece it together in your own way. This is how it should be for the reader of your story – weave background and additional information into the action, dialogue and events as you go along. If you come across ungainly dumps or clumps of information, dig them out, separate and replant them one by one.

## Collecting Clichés

We all use clichés in conversation; they are everywhere in written and spoken media; we often write them without even realising how stale and, in fact, meaningless they have become. In descriptions they fall from our lips and finger tips: 'Her face was as wrinkled as a prune'; 'He was a big, strapping lad'; 'She looked as fresh as a daisy'; 'The meadows stretched as far as the eye could see'; 'The sunlight danced on the water'; 'He gave it his all'. These similes and metaphors that have been so overused for so long have been drained of meaning and literary value.

Nitpick through your prose for any clichés, in narrative, description, dialogue (unless the character is addicted to cliché) and find either simpler or more original replacements.

## Breaking the Rules

At the start of your story, you have laid down a set of rules for the reader to operate within. They might pertain to a historical setting, where travel and communication is limited; or a futuristic world with an invented science and technology. They will be implicit in your characters, who will act according to the personalities you have drawn for them; or in external circumstances like police procedure.

If at some point in the story, in order to achieve a plot twist or your ending, you break these rules or introduce a *deus ex machina* (arbitrary 'magical' event or person), the reader will lose faith in you and interest in the plot.

Associated to breaking the rules is the no no of **Knowing Jokes** about, for instance, future or real worlds. For instance, in a historical novel do not have a character joke about how terrible it would be if women had the vote, or the impossibility of a woman prime minister. In a science fiction universe, refrain from having your cloned characters shocked at the concept of primitive human conception. They come across like the exaggerated wink to the audience of a ham actor.

## Too True to be Good

As I said in the Introduction, my first attempt at a novel was a thinly disguised tale of part of my own life. The agent I sent it to told me it was (a) boring and (b) unbelievable. 'But it can't be unbelievable,' I whined, 'It's true!' Truth and fiction are not the same thing, she snapped.

Don't make the same mistake I did by assuming that life provides stories ready made for fiction. It doesn't. I learned my lesson and my next attempt at fiction was put together around the plot structure and other information I have summarised in this book. *Blood and Water* was short-listed in the Richard and Judy How To Be Published competition and published by Macmillan New Writing.

Since then, people have often offered me real life stories that 'would make a brilliant novel', and others have come for help when they've tried to fictionalise one of their own real life experiences. Being true, though, doesn't make a story into good fiction and if you find too much co-incidental or unstructured 'truth' in yours, be ruthless and shape it back into believable fiction.

## Don't be a Wannabe

We've all read a new best-seller and thought we could have come up with a story just as good, and probably written it better, too.

Just remember that, if you've had that thought, so will a great many other would-be fiction writers, and some of them will have made the mistake of actually writing what they think is the next *Lord of the Rings, Bridget Jones' Diary, Harry Potter* or *50 Shades of Grey.*

All these books were successful because they were original in concept and execution; their authors were inventive and took risks; they weren't imitating someone else's technique or content. Your story and your style should be your own and not that of a wannabe J.K. Rowling or J.R.R. Tolkein. If you find yourself borrowing a bit of plot or slipping into the style of a favourite author, get a grip and find your own voice again – it's more likely to bring you success than being a pale imitation of someone else's.

**'I must keep my own style and go on in my own way; and though I may never succeed again in that, I am convinced that I should totally fail in any other.'**

**JANE AUSTEN**

# PART FOUR

# GETTING PUBLISHED

# 24

# FORMATTING YOUR MANUSCRIPT

Broadly speaking, there are two kinds of writers: those who write in small chunks, which they edit carefully as they go, before moving on to the next; and those whose story pours out of them from start to finish, after which they return to edit and redraft.

If you are one of the first, you will probably want to get your manuscript in the right format at the outset; if you are one of the second, you will very likely do this job at the end.

Either way, ensuring your manuscript is correctly formatted is essential if you are going to submit it to an agent, publisher or editor. Why? Because it makes your work easier to read, to assess, to mark up and, in due course, to typeset. Additionally, because there are publishing industry standards which, if you appear ignorant of them, or choose to ignore them, make you look unprofessional, unhelpful and reduce your chances of being considered as a serious author.

The guidelines I'm going to give you are the basic formatting rules for fiction manuscripts, but many agents and publishers have their own specific requirements which they make clear on their websites or in publicity material, usually as 'Submission Guidelines'. The first rule is to find, read and follow these – do not make the mistake of thinking it won't matter if you don't, or your own formatting ideas are better. You may well have to make changes, large or small, to your manuscript for each organisation you submit it to. If you want to get a foot in the door with them – just do it!

## Font

Use only one font (typeface) throughout, for all body text and headings too. Stick to a common, much used font rather than something you consider more attractive or original. If you're sending a manuscript electronically, you want to be sure the recipient has the same font on their computer, or your formatting may appear wrong to them. The two safest are Times New Roman, a serif font which some publishers prefer and may request, for fiction; and Arial, the most commonly used sans-serif typeface. Whichever one you use, stick to it – don't try to get creative by putting some sections in a different font, or trying to represent, say, handwriting with a cursive font. This is a job for a typesetter, not the author.

Whichever font you choose, the size should be 12pt and black throughout. Make headings **bold,** and emphases, titles and non-English words *italic* (do *not* <u>underline</u> – this editing convention was used in written or typewritten manuscripts to indicate what should be italicised in typeset). Do this by highlighting and using the tabs for bold and italic; do *not* change the typeface to, for instance, 'Arial Bold' or 'Times New Roman Italic'. Do not use CAPITALS for emphasis – or ***bold italics***, come to that.

## Margins, Spacing and Indentation

**Margins** should be one inch all around the page (this is the default margins setting for MS Word – the publishing industry standard software for manuscripts).

**Line-spacing** should be 1.5 (especially if your manuscript is very long) or double-spaced. (Synopses, though, are single-spaced so you can get them onto one page.)

**Paragraphs** should *either* have two line returns between them, *or* start the first line with a 0.5 inch indent, but not both. If you choose to indent paragraphs, the opening paragraph of a chapter or section should not be indented. Indents should be created with a tab, not by pressing the space bar several times. Fiction is traditionally typeset with indented paragraphs and some agents and editors like to see this in a manuscript. As an editor and publisher, I personally prefer non-indented paragraphs with a double space between them as they are easier to mark-up and make less work for a typesetter.

**Full stops/periods** should be followed by one space only – not two. Older writers, who learned on a typewriter, may have been taught to put two blank spaces after a full stop. This is no longer needed on computers, which produce more accurately spaced documents, and is not correct in manuscripts today. If you've left two spaces after every period in your story, it's simple to change in Word: click on the 'Search' boxes at the bottom right hand of your screen; click on 'Find' and type two spaces; click on 'Replace' and type one space; click on 'Replace All'.

**Line breaks** should only be made at the end of paragraphs; don't put in any hard returns in the middle of paragraphs to make a line end neatly. The whole shape and look of the manuscript will change in typeset and any interventions like this on your part will create extra work for the typesetter.

## First Page, Headers and Footers

On your cover page, which should have single line spacing, put your name and contact info on the upper left hand side of the page; genre and word count (rounded to the nearest thousand) on the upper right (both single-spaced). If you are represented by an agent, the contact details should be theirs.

**Your title**, centred and in capitals, goes a third of the way down the page; two lines below put 'by,' and two lines below that, your name.

From the second page – the start of your story – you should be in double or 1.5 line spacing.

**Chapter** headings should be in bold and can either be centred or justified to the left. The body text should be justified to the left only, leaving it 'ragged' on the right hand side. Chapters should start on a new page, but there is no need to leave a blank page between chapters.

**The Header** should start on the second page of your manuscript and should consist of, on the left, your title (or part of it, if it's very long) followed by a slash and your surname; on the right, the page number (starting from '1' on the second page).

**The Footer** can be used for a copyright assertion, best in a smaller font (8pt – 10pt), such as: *How To Write Fiction Without The Fuss* © Lucy McCarraher, October 2013.

## Dots and Dashes...

**Dots**, or ellipsis, as they are really called, which indicate an unfinished thought or, at the end of a sentence, a trailing off into silence... should be formatted like that. Three (no more) dots immediately after the last word, with a space before the next word.

**Dashes** come in two forms: en-dashes are the short ones used to hyphenate two words; em-dashes are the longer ones often used in place of brackets or to indicate speech has been broken off. (Create an em-dash in Word by typing an en-dash, immediately followed by a hard return, then a backspace to return to the end of the now longer dash.) An oft-asked question is, should there or should there not be spaces around em-dashes? In the US there is more of a preference for no spaces–like this. But in the UK, always have a space before and after an em-dash – like that.

**Quotation marks** (inverted commas) come in doubles or singles for speech and quotation. The modern preference is to use singles, 'like this', with doubles for quotes "within" quotes. Italicise (without quotation marks) the titles of books, newspapers, journals, albums and TV shows, but not the titles of songs, poems or articles, which should be unitalicised in quotation marks. Actual quotations of no more than two or three lines go within quotation marks as part of a paragraph; longer quotations form a separate, indented paragraph without quotation marks.

**Numbers** from one to nine are generally written in letters, while those from 10 upwards go in numerals.

## Consistency

Above all, be consistent in your formatting. If you are unsure of a correct, or whether to use a UK or US, spelling, make a decision and stick with it. Don't write 'OK' sometimes, 'ok' at other times, and 'okay' occasionally. Similarly, don't use double quotation marks around some dialogue and singles around others – unless you have a typographical reason to do so. Nothing drives an editor madder! Again, it makes you look unprofessional and as if you haven't bothered to consider such things.

# 25

# SUBMITTING YOUR MANUSCRIPT

Your story is the best you can make it; your manuscript is clean and professional; it's time to send your baby out into the big, wide world to seek its fortune.

Submitting your manuscript to agents who can represent you to publishers, or directly to publishers, is known as a 'query'. Whether you are querying or sending your story into writing competitions, websites, or to editors you would like to work on your manuscript, you will need to prepare two sales pitches: your synopsis and covering letter. Both these one-page items need to be crafted with care and precision; they are your story's entrée to a wider audience and if they don't announce you as an excellent writer and pique the professional reader's interest in your manuscript, you will have done yourself and your story a disservice.

Many writers feel daunted at the idea of distilling the complexities of their many thousand word story, and their own authority to write it, into a couple of short summaries, but it can and must be done. There is a formula for each and, by following them closely, you will give yourself the best chance of getting your story read.

## Agents and Publishers

First, a word about how to find and choose the right agents and publishers to send your work to.

As well as searching online, UK writers should buy the most recent copy (it comes out annually) of the *Writers' and Artists' Yearbook*. In the USA, the *Writer's Market* is similar; there is also the *Canadian Writer's Market*, the *Australian Writer's Marketplace*, etc. In other countries you will need to Google 'writers market' for the best local resources.

Read carefully the listings of book publishers and literary agents and find those that deal with your genre and format of fiction. They are usually quite specific – especially about what they do not want sent to them.

Check their websites, where you will find the authors and books they represent/publish. Note some of these that you know and like, have influenced you or that you can say your story, writing style or subject matter is similar to. Most websites will also give the name of the person responsible for/interested in your genre of story. Call and try to talk to them – if not, their PA will do, find out their name too – and ask/tell them you are submitting your work.

Take careful note of their 'submission guidelines': most will ask for a covering letter and synopsis – and they may specify the maximum length of the latter, either in words or pages. Whatever you do, stick to their individual requirements – but a one-pager is usually the minimum, and the safest and best length to stick to.

Most agents and publishers will also tell you how much of your manuscript they want you to send as a first submission: this can range from one to three chapters, up to several (specific) thousand words or, typically, the first 50 pages. Always follow these instructions to the letter, and always send the chapters, pages or word count from the start of the book (another reason I've emphasised the importance of your opening and hooking your reader). Submitting non-chronological chapters or sections that you think showcase your writing or story highlights is not a good idea. If professionals are not impressed by the opening, they know their readers won't be either.

## Covering Letter

Your covering letter should fit on a single page and follow this simple, three-paragraph format.

**Salutation**: write to the specific person you have identified – it's your call as to whether you address them by their first name, Ms/Mr… or, safest, both names.

**Paragraph 1**: introduce and summarise your story (format and genre and no more than two sentences of description). Mention why you are submitting to this agent/publisher (You represent author a and author b, whose books xxx and yyy attract a similar readership to mine/have influenced my writing/write in the same genre as I do…). If you have spoken to someone in their organisation, you can mention their name and say they advised you to write to this person.

**Paragraph 2**: Introduce yourself as a writer. You might want to say what your current employment is, especially if relevant to the subject matter. Explain why you are 'qualified' to write your book (either formal qualifications or personal experience of subject matter); be imaginative and persuasive. *Don't* talk about aspects of your life unrelated to the book (amateur pianist, mother of three). Give details of your writing background – especially any fiction you've had published online or in print, received awards or won competitions for. Do *not* quote family or friends who love your writing or story.

**Paragraph 3**: Thank them for reading your work, tell them you look forward to hearing from them and give contact details – phone numbers, email address – where they can reach you and, if appropriate, a website where they can learn more about you.

## Synopsis

Your synopsis should be written in the present tense and in the same style as your novel (literary, aimed at Young Adults, suspenseful...), but always professional and not gimmicky.

Just like your story, the opening paragraph should hook the reader and subsequent paragraphs should flow in a logical order. You can include snippets of dialogue or tiny quotes, but never hype (eg, 'In this gripping and brilliantly written scene, the reader will be on the edge of their seat as...').

Your synopsis should tell the reader:

- The title – and subtitle if you have one.

- Where and when your story is set and what theme(s) you explore.

- The main characters (three is usually enough), their quest and what stands in their way. The first time you mention a character, write their name in capitals.

- The major events and conflicts and how these are resolved – ignore subplots that are not key to the main plot.

- How the story ends. Your synopsis is not a 'teaser' for a potential buyer, and should not end on a question like, 'Bill and Tracey finally meet accidentally at the Blackpool Tower Ballroom – will the tango rekindle their desire?' Agents and publishers want to see that you know how to bring your story to a satisfying conclusion, not to be left cliff-hanging.

If you are still not sure how to make a start, go back to your story 'bible' and, instead of expanding on it, try to summarise and distill it to its essence. Try this as a format, writing a brief paragraph of approximately 100 words each under the following headings:

**The Trigger:** Describe the inciting action or event as a strong visual image; include the setting and theme so you also tell the reader the genre of your story.

**The Quest:** Introduce the main characters, their back stories (briefly) and describe their goals. Include the antagonist.

**Reversals1 & 2:** What are the first turning points created by the antagonist(s)? What conflicts occur and what action does the main character take; what decisions does she/he make that changes direction of the story?

**Reversal 3:** Describe where the main characters get to their lowest ebb, their black moment, and what they learn from this that changes them as people.

**Climax & Resolution:** What happens in the final confrontation between the protagonist and their antagonist? Give a sense of the excitement and action that takes place before… everyone lives happily ever after – or not. Who gets their just deserts? How do you tie up all the loose ends? Leave the reader with a final image portraying the hero in his/her new life and setting.

Once you have written these paragraphs, remove the headings and rewrite them so they flow as a convincing and intriguing summary of your story. If it's running over a page (or 500 words), delete unnecessary words, tighten sentences. Treat your synopsis as you have your story: get feedback from others; rewrite, edit and polish after breaks away from it.

When perfect, send out to as many agents and publishers as suit you and your story. Start writing your next project. Don't expect quick responses; call after a month (and monthly thereafter) and ask when you can expect to hear. Take rejection lightly and any feedback as gift; thank, then act on it and return to whoever gave it to you with appropriate revisions. Be persistent. Keep writing.

# ABOUT THE AUTHOR

 Lucy McCarraher started her first publishing company while she was at university, and has been publishing, editing and writing ever since. She started her working life in Australia where she edited and published magazines and books, and worked as a print and TV journalist. Back in London, she was employed as a writers' agent and as an editor for Methuen; as Director of Development at Lifetime Productions International, she developed, script-wrote and edited UK and international TV series.

Lucy became a national expert in worklife balance, writing academic and business reports for clients and authoring *The Work-Life Manual* and *The Book of Balanced Living*. As a consultant, her clients included multinational and blue chip companies, large public sector and voluntary organisations, and SMEs; she has also worked as a coach with many individuals on their work-life balance and personal development.

Her first novel, *Blood and Water,* was short-listed from 47,000 entries in the Richard and Judy How To Get Published competition, and published by Macmillan New Writing. This was followed by the sequel, *Kindred Spirits*, and *Mr Mikey's Ladies.*

Lucy's self help books include *A Simpler Life* and *The Real Secret*, both co-authored with social psychologist, Annabel Shaw. *The Real Secret* was published by Bookshaker and Lucy subsequently became the Commissioning Editor, contributing to its 140+ titles of niche business and self-development books.

She started Rethink Press Ltd in 2011 with members of the Bookshaker team, using a print-on-demand, 'supported publishing' model that allows authors with quality books in any genre to invest in the upfront costs of preparation and publication, then receive high royalties on sales. It has successfully published award-winning fiction, self-development and business books, cookbooks, travel writing and poetry. Her aim has been to provide excellent, personalised and timely author services to support writers in either presenting their work to agents or traditional publishers, self-publishing, or using the publishing services of Rethink Press.

Lucy has a post-graduate diploma in teaching Creative Writing and Literacy and is an experienced and sought-after writing coach and trainer.

**If you would like to get in touch with Lucy about your fiction writing, or any Rethink Press services, email her at lucy@rethinkpress.com and check out www.rethinkpress.com**

**For daily writing and publishing tips, links and quotes, join Lucy on www.facebook.com/rethinkpress, www.twitter.com/rethinkpress and www.pinterest.com/rethinkpress**

CPSIA information can be obtained at www.ICGtesting.com
Printed in the USA
LVOW13s1458241013

358456LV00019B/1131/P